Hooking Up

"... gives girls of all ages the in-depth information they need to know about sex, but reads like a conversation rather than a lecture. . . . This book can make an enormous contribution toward promoting the sexual health and emotional well-being of girls everywhere. . . . *Hooking Up* is bound to become a girls' cult classic—to be read at sleepovers and to sit on the coffee tables of young women's apartments. If there has ever been such a thing as an 'it' book that every girl has to own, then this is it!"

       —Diana L. Dell, MD
          Assistant Professor
          Department of Psychiatry and Behavioral Sciences
          Department of Obstetrics and Gynecology
          Duke University School of Medicine

"Delightful reading for both patients and healthcare providers! Ms. Madison's work reflects a great deal of research resulting in an accurate portrayal of information. This book is highly recommended for patients, parents, and anyone who works with young women."

       —Janice L. Bacon, MD
          President of the North American Society
          for Pediatric and Adolescent Gynecology
          Professor and Chair
          Department of Obstetrics and Gynecology
          University of South Carolina School of Medicine

"I have a personal passion for educating our young people about sex— about the joys and the risks. I am continually searching for new ways to reach them with safer sex messages. . . . *Hooking Up* is an excellent addition to my quest."

       —Margaret Higham, MD
          Medical Director of Tufts University Health Service
          Tufts University

Hooking Up

a girl's all-out guide to
SEX & SEXUALITY

amber madison

Foreword by
diana l. dell, md.
Duke University School of Medicine

Preface by
margaret higham, md,
Tufts University Health Service

 Prometheus Books

59 John Glenn Drive
Amherst, New York 14228-2197

All illustrations in this book are original drawings by Justinne Gamache.

Published 2006 by Prometheus Books

Inquiries should be addressed to
Prometheus Books
59 John Glenn Drive
Amherst, New York 14228–2197
VOICE: 716–691–0133, ext. 207
FAX: 716–564–2711
WWW.PROMETHEUSBOOKS.COM

10 09 08 07 06   5 4 3 2 1

Library of Congress Cataloging-in-Publication Data

Madison, Amber.
    Hooking up : a girl's all-out guide to sex and sexuality / Amber Madison ; foreword by Diana L. Dell.
        p. cm.
    ISBN-13: 978–1–59102–470–5 (pbk. : alk. paper)
    ISBN-10: 1–59102–470–6 (pbk. : alk. paper)
    1. Sex instruction for girls—United States. 2. Sex instruction for teenagers—United States. 3. Girls—Sexual behavior—United States.
4. Teenagers—Sexual behavior—United States. I. Title.
HQ27.5.M2103 2006
613.9071'073—dc22
                                                                2006016170

613.9071
MADI

Printed in the United States of America on acid-free paper

To my parents, who continually prove that I'll enjoy every age I will ever be.

Contents

8 Contents

Foreword

ooking Up: A Girl's All-Out Guide to Sex and Sexuality is a must-read for all young women. Amber Madison has created a hilarious and informative book that leaves no stone unturned: from bikini waxing, to condom use, to body image; if it's related to sex, it's in this book. By sharing her own stories and experiences, Amber connects with her readers and dispenses information with a comical and personal flair. Her book gives girls of all ages the in-depth information they need to know about sex, but reads like a conversation rather than a lecture.

Hooking Up includes an array of important topics about sex and sexuality, such as information about vaginas, masturbation, guys, sex acts, STDs, contraception, pregnancy, sexual assault, body image, relationships, and homosexuality. Although Amber was only twenty when she began writing this book (and thus not a doctor), all the medical information she has included is both up-to-date and medically accurate.

One of the most remarkable things about this book is that it explores sexual health issues from all angles. Instead of simply relaying physical information about sex and sexual health, it addresses the emotional aspects so often neglected in sexual information texts. Madison not only tells the reader how to use a condom, but also humorously explores what to do if a guy doesn't want to wear one and how to use one without it feeling awkward or disruptive. Her willingness to shed light on all the gritty details that constitute *real* experience is what brings this book to life and sets it apart from other available texts on the subject.

As a psychiatrist and gynecologist who has worked extensively with girls and women, I believe this book can make an enormous contribution toward promoting the sexual health and emotional well-being of girls everywhere. This book will be useful for teenagers, young women, and even parents seeking to start a dialogue with their daughters on issues concerning sex and sexuality. I have not seen another book on sexual health for young women that can claim to be both this informative—and yet this entertaining.

Through her honesty and fresh approach, Madison allows her readers to laugh at her mishaps and rejoice in her wit; all the while she teaches them how to engage in sexual activities safely and sensibly or lets them decide not to engage in any sexual activity at all. *Hooking Up* is bound to become a girls' cult classic—to be read at sleepovers and to sit on the coffee tables of young women's apartments. If there has ever been such a thing as an "it" book—one that every girl has to own—then this is it!

Diana L. Dell, MD
Assistant Professor
Department of Psychiatry and Behavioral Sciences
Department of Obstetrics and Gynecology
Duke University School of Medicine
Durham, North Carolina

I first "met" Amber Madison through reading her popular weekly sex column in the Tufts University student newspaper. Her column drew attention to sexual issues and risks in an insightful and humorous way. I was impressed with Amber's unique voice, and her ability to convey important and accurate medical information and yet still make it entertaining. When she approached me to review the accuracy of the information in this book, I was delighted to help her.

While I was in the midst of reviewing her manuscript, I happened to leave a few chapters in the back of my car. One evening as I was driving my fourteen-year-old daughter and her friend to the video store, I noticed a sudden silence in the backseat. Evidently, the girls had found the chapters and were reading away. We soon arrived at the video store, and even though I had parked the car, and turned off the radio, the girls made no move to hop out. After several silent minutes, I told the girls we were there. "Oh, we are?" my daughter asked in surprise. "Can we finish reading before we go in?"

I was struck by how absorbed they were in the manuscript. And I was impressed when, several days later, my daughter initiated a great conversation concerning one of the topics in the chapters that she had read. The book had clearly made an impact!

Hooking Up: A Girl's All-Out Guide to Sex and Sexuality is the perfect guide for young women who want to be educated about safe and responsible sex by someone who is a part of their own generation. In it, Amber speaks from her heart, including all the worries, questions, and misperceptions that she had growing up. Through her personal stories, she draws readers into her life, while simultaneously guiding them through their own. Her personal touch, candid tone, and unique sense of humor make the often-embarrassing subject of sex very accessible.

The information you will find in *Hooking Up* is medically accurate and up-to-date. Amber is very knowledgeable about sexuality and the risks of sex; her book is accurate and comprehensive and covers many topics in depth, including the expected areas, such as vaginal infections, pregnancy prevention, and sexually transmitted diseases. But it also discusses topics that are often overlooked, such as grooming one's pubic region, guys' bodily concerns, how to communicate with a partner, body image, and sexual decision making. And those issues are important too! The combination of medically accurate material presented in a fun and interesting context makes this book a needed contribution not only to bookstores but also to women's health.

As the medical director of the Tufts University Health Service, and a physician who has worked with young women for twenty-five years, I have a personal passion for educating our young people about sex—about the joys and the risks. I am continually searching for new ways to reach them with safer-sex messages that they will actually internalize. *Hooking Up* is an excellent addition to my quest.

Margaret Higham, MD
Medical Director
Tufts University Health Service
Tufts University
Medford, Massachusetts

Acknowledgments

$\mathcal{W}$hen I started writing this book, I had no idea how much help I would need along the way. I would like to extend a huge thank you to those who made this book possible, and those who kept me sane in the process.

To Alison Keehn, for giving me the guidance I needed to make this book a reality rather than a fleeting thought. To my parents, Roger Madison and Jane Leserman Madison, for teaching me to follow my own passions and for being supportive regardless of what those passions were. (A special thanks to my mom, who went above and beyond the call of duty helping me edit.) To Seth Pitman, for getting me through the rough spots, forcing me to believe in myself, and being an understanding editor. And to Meghan Gambling, for her insightful comments and helpful last-minute revisions.

To those who contributed their own stories or expertise: Ariel White, Betsy Goldman, Bonnie Cavanagh, Amanda Deibert, and those who asked that their names not be used—your voices make this book come alive.

I would also like to thank Robin Straus and Fiona Serpa, for their perseverance, and my editor, Linda Regan, for all the time and effort she dedicated to this book. To Nicole Lecht, Steven L. Mitchell, Jon Kurtz, Mark Hall, Chris Kramer, Jill Maxick, Amy King, Marcia Rogers,

Heather Ammermuller, Joe Gramlich, and everyone else at Prometheus Books, for believing in me and my manuscript. To Margaret Higham, MD, for the many conferences that helped fine-tune the medical information. Also to Diana Dell, MD; Marsha Johnson; Gail Ironson, MD; and Denniz Zolnoun, MD, for reviewing the medical content. To Edith Balbach, Francie Chew, Sheila Driscoll, Aaron and Elaine Shapiro, Jen Chenoweth, Lucia Di Poi, Andrew Gordon, and Jon Barenboim, for their assistance and advice. And finally, to my extended family, especially Robert Paushter, for being my webmaster, chart creator, and overall technical go-to man.

Introduction

I was in my grandparent's cold, musty basement when I told my mom that I had lost my virginity. My mother had her purple nightgown hiked up over her hip and was scratching her left butt cheek. Some people scratch their heads when they're thinking; my mom scratches her ass.

"You had sex? Hmmm . . ." The scratching stopped; she launched into a graphic story about losing her virginity, and that was my send-off into the sexual world.

My mother never censored or obscured our sex conversations; I *always* got the X-rated version, whether or not I wanted it. There was a time in my childhood when I wasn't allowed to see violence, but I was never too young to start hearing about sex. My parents wrote sexually explicit rap songs for their friends' birthdays, gave ties that looked like penises as Christmas presents, and casually bounced sex jokes around the dinner table. I always knew I could talk openly with my parents about sex, but I didn't always know the right questions to ask, and there were some subjects I wasn't about to discuss with either of them—it would have just been too gross.

The majority of my friends, on the other hand, were completely on their own. They couldn't talk about sex with their parents, and our school (like many in the United States) wasn't any help either. Although there were a few books available about the subject, they were dull, dry and written by someone about three times our age. The result was that our "sex education" came in bits and pieces picked up along the way: from birds-and-the-bees talks, older siblings, and the last chapters of puberty books (the ones that magically appeared on our bookshelves around the time we started to grow pubes). But regardless of where our information came from, the majority of our questions about sex were left unanswered.

We wondered, "What do you say to a guy if he doesn't want to wear a condom?" "Do you have to get a guy off once you start to hook up with him?" "Ouch! Am I really supposed to enjoy *that*?" With no place to go to find the answers to these questions, we had to learn from on-the-job training. Naturally, we all made mistakes—some that could be fixed and others that couldn't. Many of us unknowingly put ourselves at risk for pregnancy, let ourselves be convinced that we really "should" give some guy a blow job, or had multiple sexual experiences that we never actually enjoyed.

As a sex columnist at Tufts University, I learned that a lot of the sex questions we had in high school don't necessarily get answered with age and sexual experience. Even in college, most sexually active girls still don't know that the majority of people with sexually transmitted diseases don't show any symptoms or that insisting on making a guy use a condom won't make him like them any less. Perhaps this is why in the United States, two-thirds of STDs occur in young adults under twenty-five, and one out of every three girls will get pregnant before she is twenty.

As young women, we need access to straightforward sex information that answers more than just "What is a condom?" We need to know everything from "What STDs do I put myself at risk for when I give a blow job?" to "After I have sex once, will I have to sleep with every other guy I date?" Because making wise sexual choices isn't as easy as simply knowing what we *should* do, we need insight into the emotional side of sex as well as guidance through real-life sexual dilemmas.

I wanted to write this book before I got too old to remember what it's like to be a young woman baffled by sex. I've included all the facts that I wish I'd known sooner, and some of the 20/20 hindsight I gained along the way. Some of the information here may seem a bit basic because I know that sometimes the really simple questions are the most embarrassing to ask. So, to be safe, I've included everything from dealing with vaginal discharge to what to expect from sexual intercourse. I've also included a number of personal stories so that you can get a sense of the experiences I've had, and where my advice is coming from. I hope that this book gives you the information you need, and that it helps you feel more clearheaded and confident in an area that can be completely confusing.

Chapter 1

Vaginas

What the Hell?

A vagina can be annoying, and there's just no two ways around it. It bleeds, it smells, it's hairy; it's not particularly pretty, sexy, or easy to understand. Why should *it* get a starring role in *your* sex life? Your vagina *must* have lied and cheated its way in between your legs because it's clearly unqualified for the position.

But qualified or not, it's there, and you're stuck with it—like a weird hand-me-down from a distant relative. "Thanks, Great-aunt Gerta, I can really use one of these!" Yet, unlike an antique chamber pot, you can't shove a vagina to the back of your closet and forget about it. If you ever plan on being sexual, you have to become familiar and some-what comfortable with your vagina. Imagine hooking up if you aren't: "Don't get your face too close; it smells weird"; "Oh, my God, there's hair there?"; "Keep trying, baby—I *think* that's the hole."

The bottom line is that understanding what's going on with your vagina is the first step to being comfortable with sex and the key to having enjoyable sexual experiences. This chapter is about becoming familiar with all of your vagina's different parts and coming to terms with how it looks, acts, and smells.

THE WAY YOUR VAGINA LOOKS

When I came out of my mother's womb, the doctors said I was the hairiest baby they had ever seen—well, maybe not in so many words, but at least that's how I imagine it. I have always been slightly insecure and completely neurotic about how visible my dark hairs are on my pasty white skin. So when I started to grow pubic hair, I was really pissed. *More hair? You've got to be kidding me.*

When I got older and found myself in situations where someone else was going to be in contact with my pubic hair, I felt that I had to take some sort of action. But what kind of action was I supposed to take? What do most girls do with their pubic hair? Do they trim it, shave it, wax it, or just let it go au naturel? Do they take it all off just to be safe, or do they keep it all on to avoid looking prepubescent? I had no idea.

So after years of deliberation and different "hair styles," I decided to spend an afternoon doing pubic hair research. I went into Harvard Square in Cambridge, Massachusetts, with four rough sketches of different ways that a girl could keep her pubic hair.

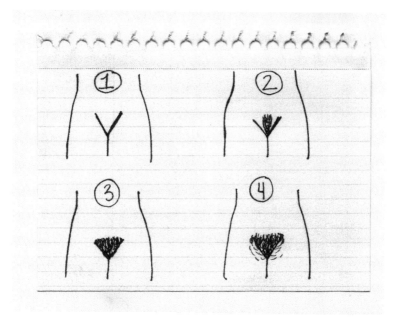

Drawing 1 represents a woman who keeps her pubic area as bald as an old man's head. Drawing 2 represents a woman who removes all her pubic hair except for a little strip in the center ("the landing strip"). Drawing 3 represents a woman who removes all the hair outside of her panty line. And drawing 4 represents a woman who doesn't groom her pubic region at all. I showed these drawings to a hundred women between the ages of sixteen and twenty-two and asked them to anonymously write down which one looked the most like their own pubic hair. These were the results:

Pubic Hair Styles of Girls 16 to 22

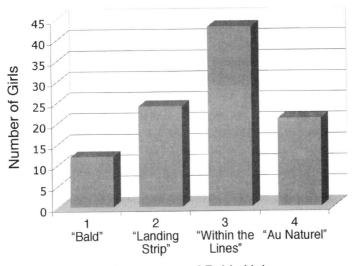

As you can see, girls do a lot of different things with their pubic hair. There is no wrong way to wear your pubes (and no right way either). If you're feeling pressure to remove your pubic hair out of fear that a guy will be grossed out if you don't, remember that pubic hair is supposed to be there; even though it may seem unsightly, it is *just hair*.

I mean, think about the hair on our heads. We obsess about how beautiful and sexy it is. We "ooooh" and "ahhhh" over someone's "gorgeous locks" and will even pet someone's "silky tresses." And yet the second a hair is growing somewhere else on our body, it's "disgusting," and it has to go. But the hair around a vagina isn't that different from the hair on a head (except it's maybe a little curlier). So if you're stressing out about your pubes, keep in mind that hair in and of itself is not overly apelike or gross; it's just that sometimes we get thrown off by the location. The bottom line with your pubic hair is that it's your vagina, so keep it as hairy (or as bald) as you like.

CHANGING THE LOOK OF YOUR VAGINA

If you decide that you want to remove some (or all) of your pubic hair, you have a few choices: hair-removal cream, shaving, or waxing. (Theoretically you could pluck the hair out with tweezers, but that could take a really long time and be pretty painful.) Shaving is definitely the easiest option. The only downsides are that the hair is only gone for a day or two, and some girls find that shaving gives them razor burn (a rashlike skin irritation). To help prevent getting razor burn, you can try running your bikini area under warm water for a few minutes before shaving and using a high-quality razor and some shaving gel.

Another hair-removal option is using a depilatory cream. Like shaving, hair-removal creams get rid of hair for only a couple of days and can also cause skin irritations. Even though the irritation will last only a day or two, the hair will be back by the time the rash is gone. If hair-removal creams and shaving irritate your skin, then you probably want to wax.

Waxing is more painful and expensive than shaving or using a cream, but it does last longer (anywhere from two to six weeks). If you want to try waxing, and you've never done it before, I would suggest going to an experienced bikini waxer. The first time that I wanted to wax, I made the mistake of trying to do it myself. It was a complete disaster. I dripped wax all over the microwave, the toaster oven, and the kitchen floor. My pubic hair looked like it was attacked by a mountain lion, and all my friends called me "mullet crotch" for the next month.

Going to a professional bikini waxer usually guarantees a good waxing job, although it can also feel a bit awkward: like the elephant in the room that no one is talking about. Here you are, chatting it up with a woman you've never met, while she pokes around your vagina and assesses your pubic hair. Some girls get paranoid that their waxer is going to be secretly grossed out or start gossiping about their pubes the second they leave the room.

If you're worried about the impression that your vaginal area will make on your waxer, you have to keep in mind how many pubic areas waxers see in their careers. There's no way that yours is going to stand out. It's not like your waxer is going to run into you at the mall and think, "Oh, I remember her—she had some intense pubes." Bikini waxers don't get grossed out or shocked; being around vaginas is their job. So they've likely seen it all.

Words from the Wise (Tips from a Bikini Waxer)

"You get the best wax if your hair is between a quarter and a half of an inch long when pulled out straight. You probably don't want to get waxed during your period because it tends to hurt more. I've done this thousands of times, so, although it may feel uncomfortable to you, I'm totally used to it."

"ALL THOSE PARTS"

Unlike guys, we aren't required to have an intimate relationship with our genitals. We don't have to hold our vaginas to ensure our piss hits the toilet. And when we look down, our genitals aren't flopping around for us to inspect. As a result, some women go a lifetime without ever touching or looking at their vagina and know it only as an upside-down triangle of hair. If you have never examined your vagina, I encourage you to take the plunge and inspect "all those parts."

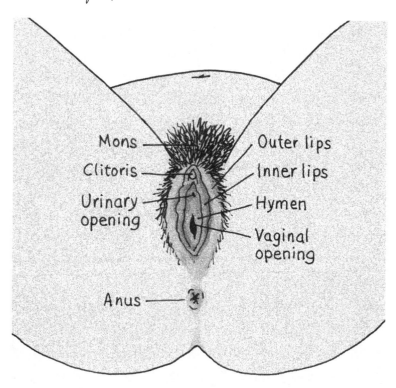

Note: *Technically, the entire area is called the "vulva." (The actual vagina is only one hole.) However, since most people use the word* vagina *to mean the whole area, in this book I use the term* vagina *to refer to the entire area as well.*

1. Mons: The cushion over your pubic bone that protects your internal organs. *Helpful hint:* If you ever decide to wax your pubic hair, removing the hair from your mons will probably be the most painful. (This is one reason that many girls leave the area untouched).

2. Outer lips/labia majora: The outer folds of skin (the hairy ones) that protect the rest of your vagina.

3. Inner lips/labia minora: The soft, fleshy, sideways-mouth-looking thing on the inside of your outer lips. *Helpful hint:* Your inner lips may be larger or smaller than your outer lips. Also, your inner or outer lips may be larger on one side than they are on the other. Everyone's vaginal lips look different, so if you have seen someone else's vagina and it looks completely different from yours, there's no need to be alarmed.

4. Clitoris: The hard spot at the top of your vagina where your inner lips come together. *Helpful hint:* The clitoris is *very* important for sexual pleasure, so make sure you figure out where yours is (most likely you'll have to direct guys there in the future).

5. Urinary opening/urethra: The hole where your pee comes out. *Helpful hint:* If bacteria get pushed into this hole, they can cause a urinary tract infection (which is often very painful). Make sure to keep this area very clean.

6. Vaginal opening: The opening to the deep hole that extends back to your uterus. (This hole is your *literal* vagina—the one a penis goes into when you have sex, and the one that blood comes out of when you're on your period.) *Helpful hint:* Because of all the flaps of skin, the opening to your vagina may not be completely obvious. Don't be alarmed if you stick your finger inside of your vagina and it feels a little chunky as opposed to completely smooth. It's natural for a vagina to have slightly protruding bumps.

7. Hymen (a.k.a. "cherry"): The layer of tissue that partially blocks your vaginal opening. *Helpful hint:* Even if you are a virgin, you may have already "popped" your hymen (a hymen doesn't actually "pop," but tears). Many girls' hymens are torn by being fingered, masturbating, using a tampon, or even falling onto the bar of a guy's bike. Some hymens bleed a lot, and others bleed only a little, so you may pop it and not even know. Some girls' hymens are so small that they don't actually "pop" at all. Either way, not having your hymen intact doesn't necessarily have anything to do with your virginity.

8. Anus: The hole where your poop comes out.

Vaginal Exploration Made Easy

✳ **Step 1: Wash your hands.** A pretty good rule of thumb: if you're going to be poking around your vagina, make sure your hands are clean. You can also use this opportunity to give yourself a pep talk in the mirror. Like getting the lyrics wrong when you're singing along with the radio, looking at your vagina is one of the few things that can feel embarrassing even if no one else is around. So assure yourself that there is nothing deranged or disgusting about exploring your own body.

✳ **Step 2: Find a private room and a mirror.** Since your vagina is underneath you, in order to look at it, you have to straddle a mirror (a task that doesn't ease the awkwardness of the activity at all). To make yourself the most comfortable, make sure that there's no chance of someone walking in on you—that *could* be very embarrassing. "Hey, Pops! I'm just exploring my vagina! Of course I washed my hands!"

✳ **Step 3: It's not an alien.** The first time you see what your vagina looks like can be a little shocking. The folds, the hair—it can look like it just stepped off a flying saucer. But don't freak out. All vaginas look a little funky if you haven't really seen one before. Yours is not deformed or especially strange; it's just a vagina.

✳ **Step 4: Figure out what's what and what's normal.** Look at the diagram of the vagina, and find each part on yourself. You might also want to make a mental note of what your vagina looks like normally. That way, you're more likely to recognize any bumps or irritations that could show up as a result of a vaginal infection or a sexually transmitted disease. (For more about what goes wrong with vaginas, see "Infections and the Gyno," p. 31, and "Sexually Transmitted Diseases," p. 87.)

The Way Your Vagina Acts

At a birthday party in seventh grade, one of my friends dared to admit that she often found a small, creamy spot in her underwear. She asked us all: "Do you guys ever notice white stuff in your underwear at the end of the day?"

We all responded immediately: "Yeah! Like when you wear dark-colored—"

"I had no idea that anyone else got that!"

"What do you guys think it *is*?"

Well, we all had noticed it, and I'm sure my friend's confession was a complete relief for everyone. I know it was for me. I thought that I wasn't wiping myself well enough when I peed or that something was leaking out of me. When I heard that other girls got white stuff in their underwear, I no longer felt like a twelve-year-old freak that needed to wear diapers.

Having "white stuff" in your underpants is completely normal. "White stuff" (discharge) is just your vagina's way of cleaning itself. And like everything else that has to do with vaginas, it varies from person to person. Your discharge may be whitish, clear, yellowish, stringy, or flaky. You may have a lot or a little. Most likely, the amount and consistency of your discharge will vary throughout the month.

When you're hooking up with someone your discharge serves as a natural lubricant, so that a finger or a penis can slide into your vagina more easily. You may be startled by how much lubrication your vagina produces when you're turned on. I remember noticing it the first few times I seriously made out with a guy—the bottom of my underwear was completely soaked. I was scared that if a guy felt it, he would think I peed in my pants.

As unnerving as "getting wet" can be, it happens to every girl when she gets sexually excited. Even if you get *really* wet and leave a little mark on a bed or a couch, it's completely normal. And you don't have to worry about what guys will think because the majority of them know what's happening and feel proud when a girl is wet (since it means he's turning her on). As for the guys who don't know, they'll have to figure it out pretty quickly or else risk being called the "idiot" who knows nothing about girls or sex. Vaginas are supposed to lubricate, so a little (or a lot) of white stuff in your panties is nothing to be self-conscious about.

THE SMELL

To me, the scariest thing about having a vagina is knowing that it has a smell. I used to freak out about the smell, and I was terrified the first few times a guy had intimate contact with my bare pubic area. What if he went around school and told everyone I had a smelly vagina? The thought was horrifying.

It's natural to assume that any smell coming from your body is a bad one because most are (the smell of your armpits, your feet, your farts, and your burps). But the smell of your vagina isn't *bad* (unless you have an infection)—it's just *a smell*.

Still, many girls believe their vagina is a dirty or disgusting place just because it has *a smell*. To mask the smell, some girls buy perfumed sprays or douches (scented water that you squirt up your vagina to "clean it out"). But any type of perfumed product that you put in your vagina can irritate the sensitive tissue and alter the pH. Altering the pH of your vagina promotes infections, and having an infection may actually cause your vagina to smell *bad*. So if you're concerned about vaginal odor, using scented products or douches is actually counterproductive. If you really want to have a perfumed pubic area, then you can try washing your pubic hair with shampoo (just don't stick the shampoo into your vagina). (For more thoughts on smell, see "When Someone Goes Down on You," p. 82.)

ACCEPTING YOUR VAGINA

Being comfortable with your vagina does not mean that you have to *love* the way it smells, or decide that it's so good looking it should grace the center of a nudie magazine. It means saying, "Sure, vaginas look a little funny, and, yeah, they have a smell, but that's OK, and that's normal." And if you didn't have a vagina, you would have a penis—which would be equally as funky. (Hey, at least we don't have to worry about hard-ons and ejaculation.)

The more familiar you are with your vagina, the less scary it seems. And there's no reason for you to be freaked out, grossed out, or embarrassed by part of your own body. Whatever may bother you about your vagina, remember that it's what makes your sex life possible. So if you're interested in sex, you have to be interested in your vagina.

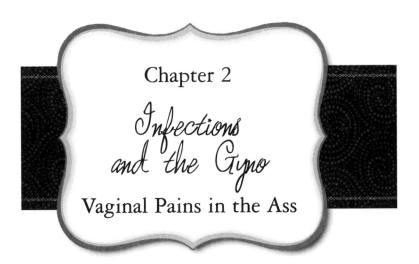

Chapter 2

Infections and the Gyno

Vaginal Pains in the Ass

*M*y first yeast infection was somewhat of a family affair. I was traveling around the Northeast with my parents looking at colleges, and in the middle of some tour guide's long-winded speech about how great Ithaca was, I began to notice that something was wrong. It felt like I had poison ivy in my vagina. I tried to play it cool by hanging toward the back of the group and discreetly scratching myself, but my parents kept trying to push me to the front to ask questions. I didn't have any questions because I knew there was no way I would ever go to a school where the campus population might recognize me as "that crotch scratcher."

I kept waiting for the itching to stop. It didn't. I showered, and it stung. I had no choice but to ask my mother what was wrong with me.

"Hey, Mom, I, uh, my vagina . . . well, it's kinda itchy. What do you think is wrong with me? Could I have a yeast infection?"

"Well, how's your discharge?"

"My discharge?"

"On your underwear. Is it chunkier than usual?"

"I don't know. I don't *usually* measure the consistency of my discharge."

"Well, does it smell funny?"

"Funny how?"

"You know, it's been so long since I've had a yeast infection . . .

Roger!" she yelled to my dad in the other room. "Amber thinks she has a yeast infection. Do you remember what it smells like?"

"It smells yeasty!" he yelled back.

"Yeasty," my mom repeated, just in case I hadn't heard him.

Not only was "yeasty" completely useless information, but I also had to have the mental image of my father's nose being finely tuned to the stench of my mother's vaginal yeast. Awesome.

As for my situation, we decided to wait it out a day to see what would happen. When it didn't get any better, my mom decided that I might as well pick up some medication, a chore that she announced publicly when we were in the car with my uncle. We found a drugstore, and *all* got out of the car. I bought my first box of Monistat 3 with my mother, my father, and my uncle, all there for moral support.

Vaginas get infected easily. That's just another one of those things that you have to deal with when you're a girl. You can take precautions to help prevent infections, but most girls will get some kind of vaginal infection (vaginitis) eventually. Being able to recognize the signs of the major types of vaginitis will help you identify an infection if you get one (although only your doctor can tell for sure). Knowing that a specific symptom is likely the result of a vaginal infection can help you remain calm if you suddenly start experiencing vaginal troubles. This chapter is about vaginal health: the different types of vaginal infections, what you can do to prevent them, and what to expect from a visit to the gynecologist.

YEAST INFECTIONS

What it is. A yeast infection is an overgrowth of a fungus that's naturally present in your vagina.

What it feels like. When you have a yeast infection, the inside or outside of your vagina may itch, burn, or feel sore.

Other signs of infection. You may also notice that your discharge is thick, even to the point that it's lumpy (like cottage cheese). Some girls notice their discharge smells "yeasty," like bread rising or raw dough.

Getting diagnosed. Some common sexually transmitted diseases (STDs) have symptoms that are similar to yeast infections. If you have had a yeast infection before, you can probably diagnose yourself and buy the correct over-the-counter medication. If you haven't and don't know exactly what it's like, it's best to have a doctor give you a definitive test. In general, if you want to be absolutely positive that you have a yeast infection, or you want to treat it with a prescription pill, you must see a doctor.

Treatment (important!). If you decide to buy over-the-counter medication to treat your yeast infection, you'll find many options. There are one-day, three-day, and seven-day cream treatments, all of which you insert into your vagina like a tampon. As tempting as it may be to buy the one-day—because why wait a week to cure an infection that could be gone in a day?—I would actually advise against it.

My junior year in college I made the mistake of buying the one-day cream. It stung so much that, fifteen minutes after inserting the medication, I was naked in the bathtub, frantically splashing water between my legs. I spent two hours trying anything I could think of to make the pain go away. When my housemate came home from the library at one in the morning, she caught me naked on my floor straddling her desk fan.

Not only can the one-day cream cause irritation, but also it's significantly less effective than other treatment options. The three-day treatment is your best choice. The infection is treated fairly quickly, and the medication won't send most girls running for the faucet. If you find that the three-day medication is irritating, try the seven-day treatment. Just make sure that you read the instructions and insert the medication *right* before you're going to bed. That way, the medication has a chance to mix with your vaginal fluids and is less likely to irritate you when it finally drips out in the morning.

What can cause it. Although some yeast infections arise without any kind of specific cause, there are some factors that can make you more likely to get one. You're more likely to get a yeast infection if you're about to get your period, you're taking antibiotics, you're going on or off birth control pills, or you're spending a lot of time in a bathing suit, a leotard, or any type of tight or noncotton underwear. In addition, some girls are naturally more susceptible to getting yeast infections than others.

What can help prevent it. L. Acidophilus (a good bacteria that's already present in your intestinal tract) helps keep the yeast in your vagina at a normal level. One of the best ways to prevent a yeast infection is to take *L. Acidophilus* pills or eat a lot of yogurt (with live, active *Acidophilus* cultures). Another good way to protect yourself from getting a yeast infection is to wear loose-fitting cotton underwear as much as possible.

Suck factor. On a scale of one to ten on the suckiness continuum, having a yeast infection sucks between a three and a five. Like the kid who sits next to you and pops his gum, it's constantly annoying, but it doesn't have to completely ruin your day.

Sex and yeast infections. If you have a yeast infection, you should wait until you have gone through the full treatment and your symptoms are gone before you have sex. (Besides, if you have sex before that, it's not going to feel very good anyway.) Although technically yeast infections aren't considered sexually transmitted diseases, you can give one to a guy if you have unprotected sex. Also, some condoms are lubricated with substances that can irritate or even feed an infection. And some yeast infection treatments weaken the latex of the condom, making it more likely to break.

Important note. If you are still having symptoms after you have finished your full treatment, you should go to a doctor to find out if your symptoms are being caused by something else (e.g., a sexually transmitted disease).

BACTERIAL VAGINOSIS

What it is. Bacterial vaginosis is an overgrowth of bacteria in your vagina. It is one of the most common vaginal infections.

What it feels like. About a third of girls with bacterial vaginosis experience itching and burning. The rest don't notice anything.

Other signs of infection. The main sign of this infection is a foul, "fishy"-smelling odor that may get worse after sex. If you have bacterial vaginosis, you may also notice a gray-white milky discharge.

Getting diagnosed. Because one of the main symptoms of bacterial vaginosis is smell, many girls don't see a doctor because they're too embarrassed. Understandably, no one wants to greet her physician with "Doc, my vagina smells really bad. Is there something wrong?" But you have to see a doctor to have the infection diagnosed and treated. And really, doctors have seen many cases of bacterial vaginosis; yours isn't going to gross them out at all.

Treatment. Bacterial vaginosis can be cured only through a cream or pill that your doctor prescribes. If you don't get your infection treated, you increase your likelihood of getting more serious infections that could damage your reproductive system.

What can cause it. It's not totally clear what causes bacterial vaginosis, but it seems to be associated with having unprotected sex and douching.

What can help prevent it. To help prevent getting bacterial vaginosis, don't douche, and wear a condom if you have sex (semen can feed the bacteria that cause the infection).

Suck factor. On a scale from one to ten on the suckiness continuum, having bacterial vaginosis sucks at about a five. The symptoms may not be that uncomfortable, but anything that can cause serious damage if it isn't treated is pretty crappy.

Sex and bacterial vaginosis. Bacterial vaginosis cannot be passed to a partner, but you shouldn't have sex until you have finished treating your infection. Having sex before your infection has gone away can make it last longer.

TRICHOMONIASIS

What it is. Trichomoniasis is a vaginal infection caused by a parasite. This parasite is sexually transmitted.

What it feels like. Some girls with trichomoniasis experience itching or burning in the vaginal area, and many girls don't feel anything at all.

Other signs of infection. Some girls notice that they have more discharge than normal, and that their discharge is bubbly, greenish, or grayish, and may smell bad.

Getting diagnosed. To get diagnosed with trichomoniasis, you have to go to your doctor and get a pelvic exam.

Treatment. Usually doctors prescribe a single pill or a course of antibiotics to treat trichomoniasis. Because the parasite is sexually transmitted, it's important that any sexual partners you may have get treated at the same time (even if they don't think they have it—most guys who have trichomoniasis don't have any symptoms).

What can cause it. You can get trichomoniasis by having unprotected sex with someone who is infected.

What can help prevent it. To prevent getting trichomoniasis, use a condom every time you have sex.

Suck factor. On a scale from one to ten on the suckiness continuum, having trichomoniasis sucks between a two and a four, depending upon the severity of your symptoms. Because it won't cause any long-term damage, it's not a huge deal if you're infected, but having an active trichomoniasis infection may make you more vulnerable to contracting HIV if you are exposed to the virus.

Sex and trichomoniasis. Because trichomoniasis is sexually transmitted, it's important that you don't have sex until both you and your partner have finished taking your medications. Otherwise, you could keep passing the parasite back and forth.

URINARY TRACT INFECTION

What it is. A urinary tract infection (UTI) occurs when bacteria get into your urinary tract and multiply.

What it feels like. A urinary tract infection is probably one of the most uncomfortable things that can happen to your vaginal area. It feels like you constantly have to pee, even if you have just finished going and have nothing left to urinate. And every time you do pee, it burns like hell (not a little icy-hot burn, but like someone has lit a giant bonfire and your panties are the kindling).

Other signs of infection. Another sign that you may have a UTI is that you have blood in your urine (and you're not on your period).

Getting diagnosed. If you are having symptoms of a urinary tract infection, you will want to see the doctor as soon as possible because some infections can get more uncomfortable and more serious very rapidly. Once you're at the doctor's office, all you have to do to get tested for a UTI is pee in a cup.

Treatment. The treatment for urinary tract infections is a course of antibiotics. The antibiotics should help you feel much better in as little as twelve hours. While you're waiting for the antibiotics to kick in, you can take Uristat (which you can buy at most drugstores). It will make your pee turn bright orange, but it will also take away the majority of your symptoms.

Although Uristat may take away much of your discomfort, it doesn't treat the infection. Since the infection may get worse quickly, don't use Uristat as a way to delay going to the doctor. The more severe your symptoms become, the less effective Uristat will be.

What can cause it. Urinary tract infections are caused by bacteria from your anus getting pushed up your urethra (i.e., butt germs getting pushed up your pee hole). Girls who are having sexual intercourse (vaginal sex) are more likely to get urinary tract infections than girls who aren't. However, UTIs can happen to anyone.

What can help prevent it. To prevent getting urinary tract infections, always wipe yourself from front to back when you go number two, and never let anything that has been in close contact with your anus come anywhere near your vagina. It can also help if you pee immediately after sex. That way, if some bacteria got pushed up your urethra, your pee will wash it out.

Suck factor. On the suckiness scale from one to ten, having a urinary tract infection sucks between a six and a nine (depending on how bad your symptoms are). UTIs can be very painful. So when people tell you to avoid letting anything that's been in contact with your butt get near your vagina, they aren't screwing around.

Sex and urinary tract infections. If you have been diagnosed with a urinary tract infection, don't have sex until you have finished your antibiotics.

TIPS FOR PREVENTING VAGINITIS

✳ **Take it easy with the thongs.** It's not totally clear whether thong underwear promotes vaginal infections. But many women who are part of the "thongs are permanent wedgies" camp seem to think that "they just can't be good for you." I have heard that thongs can be a miniature slide for the bacteria from your butt to get to your vagina, and that the edges of thongs can irritate your outer vaginal lips. To be on the safe side, wear a thong only if you really think it's necessary. If you're lounging around your house or going to bed, just change into granny panties.

✳ **Wear cotton.** Although cotton isn't the sexiest fabric in the world, it's the "healthiest" underwear fabric because it can absorb moisture, and it allows air to move through it. When you're buying underwear, make sure that at least the crotch area has a cotton insert (and most should), even if the rest of it is made out of something slinkier.

✳ **Wear loose-fitting clothing when possible.** It's impossible (as well as unnecessary) to avoid tight clothing all together. But when you're wearing tight clothes (be it a leotard, a bathing suit, or pants), it's a good idea to change out of them as soon as it's convenient.

✳ **Go commando.** Infections thrive in moist, dark places (an environment that underwear creates). Going underwear-free and letting your vagina "air out" is a good way to prevent infections. Unless you're feeling daring and want to go to school without panties on, the best time to go commando is when you're sleeping. Try spending a few nights a week wearing just your pajamas without underwear.

✳ **Don't go crazy washing.** It's important to wash yourself every day, but it's counterproductive to douse your vagina with soap and vigorously scrub around. The best way to clean yourself is with a little soap on the outside of your vaginal area and a lot of water (don't dig up there with soapy fingers). Use a gentle soap that doesn't have dyes or perfumes, and make sure that you thoroughly rinse the soap out. Your vagina actually cleans itself (which is why you have discharge), so adding a lot of soap to the mix disrupts the natural pH and can cause an infection.

✳ **Always wipe front to back.** When you go number two, always wipe yourself from front to back. That way, your butt germs will have less of an opportunity to reach your vagina, helping prevent urinary tract infections.

THE PELVIC EXAM

If you think that you have a vaginal infection, an STD, or you just need an annual Pap smear (recommended for sexually active women and women over twenty-one), you will need to have a pelvic exam. There is nothing quite like the experience of visiting a gynecologist and having her latex-covered hands probe your vagina. But as strange and somewhat violating as a pelvic exam may feel, getting one could save your life.

During a pelvic exam, you may be tested for various vaginal infections or STDs, and you will get a Pap smear. A Pap smear is the only way to test for signs of cervical cancer (a cancer that can affect women under thirty). If precancerous cells are detected early (through regular Pap

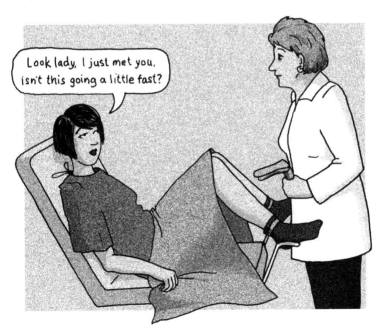

smears), actually developing cervical cancer is completely preventable. If cervical cancer is not caught early, it is much more serious and potentially life threatening.

Either your doctor or a gynecologist can give you a pelvic exam. Many girls feel the most comfortable having a woman perform the exam (whether she's your regular physician or a gynecologist). During the exam, you'll be completely naked except for a paper gown and a sheet over your lap. You'll lie on an examination table with your legs spread apart and your feet up in stirrups. It's a pretty awkward position (you kinda look like a frog), but you only stay there for a few minutes.

When the exam begins, a doctor or nurse will stick a finger inside of your vagina to feel around for anything abnormal. Then, your examiner will stick an instrument called a speculum (which looks like duck lips) into your vaginal opening. When the speculum is inside of you, the doctor will open it slightly. It may make a startling clicking sound, but the opening of the speculum doesn't actually hurt. The physician will then take a long, plastic brush and stick it into your vaginal opening to swab some cells from your cervix (the entrance to your womb at the back of your vagina). That part feels like a little pinch, but it takes just a second.

Since you're already naked and in the stirrups, you may want to go ahead and get tested for STDs. Before your exam, talk to your doctor about your sexual history, and your doctor can determine which STDs you should be tested for (if any). Most STD tests are as simple as having your cervix swabbed with a long Q-tip (which shouldn't be very painful).

The hardest part of a pelvic exam isn't so much the physical discomfort as it is the psychological discomfort. Having a doctor's face in between your legs for five minutes isn't anyone's idea of a good time. So if after a pelvic exam you feel a little embarrassed or disturbed, it's totally normal. It always helps me to remember that doctors do thousands of pelvic exams in their careers and don't think twice about being just inches away from full-frontal nudity. As awkward as a pelvic exam may feel for you, to a doctor it's another day, another vagina.

Q&A with Family Nurse Practitioner Bonnie Cavanagh
(She has seen more college girls' vaginas than Colin Farrell has.)

Q. Judging from the vaginas that you have seen, what do most girls do with their pubic hair?

A. I would say it's 50/50. Half of them are partially or fully shaved or waxed, and the other half haven't done anything.

Q. Do you have a pubic hair preference? Would you rather a woman shave to get all the hair out of the way?

A. I actually prefer that women don't do anything with their pubic hair. When women shave, their hair follicles can get infected— which can be pretty painful. You know, in Europe, a lot of women don't even shave their legs or armpits. In this country, we have such fixed notions about what vaginas should look like. We're bombarded with all sorts of douche and vaginal products that claim the vagina is unclean. And that's just not true. The products that claim to "clean out the vagina" really just promote infections.

Q. Any advice for someone who is about to get her first pelvic exam?

A. If you're not sexually active but want to get a prescription for birth control pills to help clear up your skin or make your period more regular, then you don't need to get a pelvic exam. You don't actually *need* a pelvic exam until you're having sexual intercourse (or turn twenty-one—whichever comes first). And after that, you should get one every year.

    If you're nervous about getting a pelvic exam, tell your practitioner. Ask her any questions you have ahead of time, and have her tell you what she's going to do before she does it. Many girls worry about getting pelvic exams because they've heard from their friends that pelvic exams are painful. But pelvic exams shouldn't be too uncomfortable. If something is hurting you, or you want your doctor to tell you more about what she's doing or what she's seeing, don't be afraid to speak up.

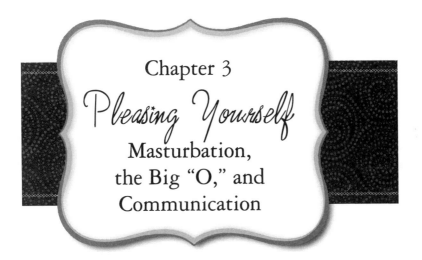

Chapter 3

Pleasing Yourself
Masturbation, the Big "O," and Communication

J was fifteen and had never used a tampon the first time I was fingered. My friend's parents were out of town and, with a couple of well-crafted lies, I managed to spend the night at her house with my first real boyfriend. We slept on a pullout bed that reeked of wet dog, but the mattress could have been drenched in urine and the night still would have seemed every bit as magical.

He kissed me softly at first, then his kisses turned deep and hard as though his mouth were desperately seeking the acceptance of my soul. Left hand cupped over my still-developing breast, he kissed slowly down the side of my neck. Ever so delicately, he slid the blue velour panties from my bony hips, down my legs, until they reached my ankles. . . .

BAM! Two thick fingers with uncut nails forced themselves into my fragile vagina. I screamed and snapped my legs shut. It felt about as unnatural as shoving a potato up my nostril, except it sure as hell wasn't my nostril that was throbbing with pain.

Painful as it was, at least my boyfriend was able to find the hole. I remember a kid in eighth grade who was bragging about fingering a girl; he told *everyone* that she had an "extremely tight pussy." As it turned out, he had completely missed her vagina and was trying to put his fingers into a nonexistent hole in her groin.

I also remember a guy on my bus the first day of high school who warned me against getting my "clete-ooor-e-us" pierced. "Cli-to-ris" = an organ that gives girls sexual pleasure. "Clete-ooor-e-us" = a type of dinosaur?

The point is, the majority of teenage boys know very little about vaginas. Even if they can find the general area and correctly name the parts, they probably don't know what sorts of motions give a girl pleasure. This wouldn't be a problem if girls knew their own bodies and could teach guys what to do. But, unfortunately, that rarely seems to be the case. It's like guys are trying to learn how to drive from instructors who don't know the gas pedal from the brake.

You can't blame a guy for not knowing how to please you if you don't even know how to please yourself. This chapter is about learning how to give yourself pleasure in the hope that it will give you a greater sense of control over your sexual experiences.

MASTURBATION

When I was younger, I thought that there was something very wrong about masturbating. Every time I did it, I felt guilty, dirty, and ashamed. I wanted to stop masturbating, but it felt good, so I usually gave in.

I was mortified by the fact that I masturbated. I remember when my grandfather died I was scared that he really was "looking down on us" and would be able to see what I was doing. I was convinced that my masturbation secret would be one that I would take with me to my grave.

When all of my guy friends started talking about how they masturbated, I kept my mouth shut.

"Dude, I was home alone yesterday, and I jerked off seven times. Hah. Seven."

"Yeah, the other day, I got a sore spot on my dick from yanking it too hard."

"Well," I said, "I don't masturbate. I think it's kind of a guy thing."

And even when a female friend of mine admitted to masturbating with a paintbrush, I still wouldn't fess up.

"I was reading a romance novel in the bathtub and got horny, so I put a paintbrush up my vagina."

"Yeah," I said. "I could never do that. I can't even use a tampon."

It took me years to admit that I, too, was a masturbator, and that (even more incriminating) I had been masturbating since before I even knew what masturbation was.

As a girl, it can be hard to talk about masturbation, even though many guys talk about it all the time. Maybe it's easier for guys to talk about because they have eight thousand cool nicknames for masturbating. They get to brag about jacking off, whacking off, jerking off, beating off, choking the lizard, or spanking the monkey. Meanwhile, we have to talk about how we "masturbated," which just sounds a little too technical to be cool.

For many people, the idea of girls masturbating seems more taboo than guys masturbating. Maybe since we aren't used to seeing girls fondle their crotches like guys do, touching ourselves seems wrong. Guys get to go around grabbing their genitals whenever they feel the need. They adjust their "package," scratch themselves in public, and somehow get away with sitting for hours with their hands down their pants. Girls, on the other hand, could never reach down their pants to adjust their labia because it's "not very ladylike." But just because messing around with our vaginas isn't accepted public behavior, it doesn't mean that we shouldn't masturbate, that we don't masturbate, or that it's gross if we do.

Whether or not girls talk about it, many do masturbate. Athletes, brainiacs, girls who have boyfriends, girls who are single, you name it—they're all touching themselves. Some start when they're very young, and others don't try it until they're older. But nearly all women masturbate eventually.

Masturbation is completely normal, and any way that a girl goes about masturbating is normal as well. Girls masturbate in many different ways, all of which are totally legitimate. I've heard of girls using couches, pillows, stuffed animals, paintbrushes, detachable showerheads, or streaming water. Masturbating is nothing to be ashamed of or feel dirty about. Touching yourself is the best way to figure out what gives your body pleasure. And knowing that will give you a greater sense of control during your sexual encounters.

YOUR VAGINA, YOUR CLITORIS, AND SEXUAL PLEASURE

Many people have a skewed view of how "most girls" masturbate. I remember there were always rumors going around my high school about how some girl had masturbated with a frozen hot dog, and some other girl had masturbated with a field hockey stick. It made sense to most people that girls should masturbate by sticking anything slightly penis-like into their vagina. It seemed logical that if guys mimic sexual intercourse (vaginal sex) when they masturbate, then girls should, too.

Most girls, however, find that trying to masturbate only by moving something in and out of their vagina is not very successful. Although it's true that some girls give themselves pleasure by sticking things into their vagina (but hopefully nothing as dirty or rough as a field hockey stick), many girls' masturbatory lives take place without any penetration. While the vagina obviously plays a big role in sex, it doesn't play that big of a role in pleasure. The organ that gives most women sexual pleasure is the clitoris (pronounced either "clit-AH-ris" or "cli-TOR-us").

In early high school, the clitoris is somewhat like Bermuda: sure, everyone's heard of it, but not many people actually know where it is. And even those who figure out how to get there probably aren't totally sure why to even bother. As much as you may hear about "rubbin' on yo' clit" in risqué rap songs, it's not clear how important a part the clitoris plays in a woman's sexual pleasure—but the part it plays is huge. According to a survey by *Glamour* magazine, nearly two-thirds of all women can have an orgasm only if their clitoris is stimulated. Even girls who do have orgasms through penetration probably climax only because their clitoris is being indirectly rubbed.

The clitoris is simply a bundle of nerve endings that's very sensitive to touch. You can find it by feeling for a small bump at the top of your inner labia. (If you're having trouble finding it, you may want to refer back to the diagram of the vagina on p. 24.) Once you find your clitoris, you can try touching it in different ways to see what feels good to you. Since the clitoris is a very sensitive organ, be delicate—don't just start banging it around. If it begins to get sore, you may be rubbing it a bit too vigorously.

The importance of the clitoris may at first seem like a bit of a downer as far as sex is concerned. It makes the issue of having an orgasm from sexual intercourse a little more complicated than "in and out." Our whole lives we hear about the great orgasms women experience while having sex, but we generally aren't informed that those orgasms were a result of clitoral stimulation, not just vaginal penetration. You may look at this as one more reason to delay sexual intercourse. After all, it's the "everything but" sex acts—the ones that take place outside of the vagina —that are most likely to give a girl an orgasm.

This is not to say that the vagina offers no pleasure at all. Many women do find orgasms more pleasurable when there's something inside of their vagina. Others find they have a sensitive place called the "G spot"—although some people question whether this spot actually exists. The G spot" (if it does exist) is located about two inches up the vagina, toward the front of the body. Those who find the spot pleasurable to touch may have better orgasms when it is stimulated.

Every girl has different ways of pleasing herself. What works for you may not be the same thing that works for your friends. You really have to do your own exploration to find out what feels best for your body. While in the process of figuring this out, don't ignore your vaginal hole, but don't get tricked into thinking it's the be-all or end-all solution for sexual pleasure either. If you're experiencing trouble having an orgasm, then your clitoris is definitely worth checking out.

USING A VIBRATOR

I used to be totally against vibrators. The way I saw it, using a vibrator to masturbate instead of your hands was the same as the difference between driving a car that's an automatic and driving one that's a stick. My whole driving life I had been behind the wheel of a '93 stick-shift, and I took great pride in how well I knew my car. I knew by merely looking at a hill if I could take it in fifth, or if I had to downshift to fourth. I knew that when I ran the AC, it needed a little extra gas to keep from stalling out, and I knew to the nearest foot how far it could roll in neutral. I was convinced that no girl who drove an automatic truly knew her car in the same way I did and that no girl who masturbated with a vibrator truly knew her body as well as someone who used her hands.

But then my friends started talking about how they were finally able to have an orgasm because they used a vibrator. They told me that having orgasms from a vibrator gave them more confidence that they could have an orgasm with a partner. So I changed my mind about being antivibrator (although I do still think that knowing how to use your hands is important). The thing about vibrators is that they make masturbation very easy. Especially for girls who are having trouble figuring out how to please themselves, a vibrator can be really helpful.

You may not be thrilled by the prospect of getting a vibrator; after all, having one can feel like quite an admission. Actually owning a vibrator can feel like the tipping point between being someone who masturbates and someone who *is a masturbator*. It's a declaration of "Yeah, I've masturbated in the past—and you can bet that I'll do it again in the future!" And for many girls, that's a pretty scary confession to make.

But with as much emotional baggage that may come along with having a vibrator, buying one really isn't a big deal. If you think you'll feel strange about people knowing that you have one, then don't tell anybody. Getting a vibrator is not a long-term commitment or huge investment. It's not like you're buying a two-thousand-dollar Chihuahua that you'll be stuck with for fifteen years. If you buy a vibrator, and after a week you're still horrendously uncomfortable knowing that you own it, then go bury it in the neighbor's trash can.

Vibrators can be a great way to give yourself pleasure (especially if you're having trouble having an orgasm). But think of vibrators the same way you would think of gutter guards in a bowling alley: they make it easier if you're a beginner, but eventually you have to play a real game. Don't let owning a vibrator get in the way of figuring out how to please yourself with your own hands. After all, you're not going to take your vibrator with you every time you hook up with someone.

HAVING AN ORGASM

Orgasms feel really good, and having one is probably something you'd like to experience if you haven't already. Physically, an orgasm is just the contraction of your uterus, vaginal walls, and anus all at the same time.

The sensation of an orgasm is something that women describe in different ways. Some say an orgasm feels like a tightening followed by a releasing or the relief of a built-up tension. Others say it's like an explosion or a series of tremors. And some say it feels like a sneeze.

Because it's difficult to put into words what an orgasm feels like, many girls wonder if they've ever had one. But if you're not sure about whether or not you've had an orgasm, you probably haven't. As difficult as it is to verbalize what an orgasm feels like, you'll know when it happens. When you have an orgasm, you know instantly, "That was it."

If you're experiencing trouble getting off, the best thing you can do is stay focused and relaxed in sexual situations (either alone or with a partner). You can't have an orgasm if you're thinking about your homework or pondering your future. You also can't have an orgasm if you feel tense or self-conscious. This may mean that you'll find it easier to learn to have one on your own. Although being with a guy may help you to stay in the moment, it's pretty hard to be relaxed if he's been diligently trying to please you and nothing is happening.

If you can give yourself an orgasm on your own, you can then teach your partner what to do later. Consistently being able to give yourself an orgasm will boost your "orgasmic confidence." The less worried you are about being able to have an orgasm when you go into a sexual encounter, the easier it will be to actually have one.

Many women don't have their first orgasm until sometime in their twenties. So if you're having trouble, it's probably completely normal. However, there are some physical conditions, including diabetes and thyroid disorders, that can make it difficult for a girl to have an orgasm. Other factors, such as feeling guilty or anxious about sex, having a poor body image, or taking medications (especially antidepressants) may also affect your sexual fulfillment. If any of the factors listed in this paragraph apply to you, and you're experiencing difficulty having an orgasm, you may want to talk to your doctor, a counselor, or a psychiatrist. Very often, one of these professionals will be able to help you with your problem.

Orgasms are very pleasurable, and no one who is sexually active is going to tell you that they're an unimportant part of sex. But as wonderful as they are, the pressure to have one (either because you want one, or your partner wants you to have one) can sometimes be overwhelming.

If all you're thinking about is having an orgasm, it can completely ruin other parts of a sexual encounter. It's counterproductive to make sexual experiences so goal-oriented that you don't enjoy them. The best way to approach having orgasms is that it's great if they happen, but it's okay if they don't.

FAKING IT

Even though everyone tells you not to, it can be tempting to fake an orgasm. Difficulty getting off, as well as pressure to look like you're enjoying a sexual encounter, can make faking an orgasm a more alluring alternative than explaining to your partner that it's not going to happen. Maybe you don't want the guy you're with to feel inadequate, or you want him to feel extra turned on hearing you get off. For one reason or another, nearly every girl fakes an orgasm at some point in her life. So if you have, it's nothing to beat yourself up over. If you do it regularly, however, you may want to think about why.

If you're in the habit of faking orgasms, two questions you should consider are: why aren't you having an orgasm? and why aren't you telling your partner? If you find it difficult to have an orgasm when masturbating, then it's not surprising that you're experiencing difficulty having one with a partner as well. But if you *are* able to have one on your own (and can't with your partner), then he's probably not stimulating you the right way—and if he is, then you're not comfortable enough with him to get off. Because having an orgasm means letting go of yourself for a moment, it's often hard to have one unless you're with someone you totally trust.

Aside from why you're not getting off, you should consider why you're pretending that you are. Some girls don't talk about their difficulties having an orgasm because they're afraid that their partner will get frustrated. Some are even concerned that a guy will leave or cheat if he thinks that he's not being enjoyed sexually. And many girls worry about making their partner feel like a bad lover.

As difficult as it is to talk to a guy about not reaching an orgasm, if you communicate your problem in the right way (and the guy isn't a total ass), there's nothing to worry about. Explain to your partner that vaginas are complicated, and that he isn't a failure if he doesn't figure you out right away or get it right 100 percent of the time. Let him know what he could do better, but also make it clear that you enjoy hooking up with him, even if you don't get off.

If you are truly comfortable with a guy, you should be able to tell him that you're not having orgasms. If you don't feel like you can assert yourself in a relationship, then maybe there are some trust and security issues that you should work out with your partner. Or perhaps you're just involved with the wrong guy. Sexual experiences should be enjoyable for both people involved, so don't get so wrapped up in your partner's experience or his ego that you neglect your own satisfaction.

COMMUNICATING WHAT *REALLY* WORKS

Once you've figured out what gives you pleasure and what gets you off, it's important to share the information with your partner. Good verbal communication is the key to a healthy and satisfying sex life. You can't expect your partner to read your mind or interpret your sounds. Guys may not know the difference between your good "ahhhhhh" and your bad "ahhhhhh." A moan that may mean "ouch" to you could mean "orgasm" to him. If you want your partner to know how to please you, you have to let him know what feels good and what doesn't.

Don't worry about offending a guy by giving him directions because the majority of guys aren't put off by girls telling them what to do. In a survey given by *Cosmopolitan* magazine to fifteen thousand guys, only 1 percent said that they would rather a girl fake it if she isn't enjoying a sexual encounter. The other 99 percent said that they wanted feedback about what to do to make the experience more pleasurable. So don't stay quiet about how a guy can please you because you're afraid of hurting his feelings; *guys want to know how to give girls orgasms.*

The best way to let a guy know what's working and what isn't is by telling him as he is doing it. Say, "That feels good," or "Keep doing that," or "That kinda hurts." If you want a more hands-on approach, you can guide his hand and show him what to do. And if you're not comfortable with giving him tips in the middle of the action, then bring it up after you finish hooking up. You're not going to insult a guy if you start your advice with, "I like it when . . . ," or "It feels best when . . ." As long as you don't start the conversation with, "It really sucks when . . . ," he'll be fine.

Because guys want to know how to please girls, there isn't any wrong way to give them directions (assuming that you're not rude about it). Once I was even bold enough to stop a guy mid-hookup, draw a labeled diagram of the vagina, and say, "This is the clitoris, touch this." I don't necessarily recommend doing that—I realize in retrospect that move was a little insensitive and bizarre. But as odd as it may have been, the guy wasn't offended or weirded out. Sure, giving directions might feel a little awkward at the time, but letting a guy know what to do will make your sexual experiences much more pleasurable. And if you're hooking up with someone, you should be enjoying it.

"When Sarah's boyfriend wasn't pleasing her the right way, she decided to leave him a hint."

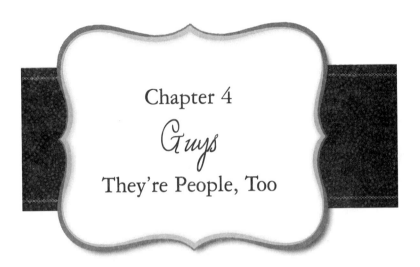

Chapter 4
Guys
They're People, Too

The entirety of my first relationship took place inside a multiplex movie theater by my house. From September through December my freshman year in high school, I spent every Saturday afternoon sitting nervously next to my boyfriend pretending to be *really* into whatever movie we had decided to see. I never actually knew what was going on in the film because I was too preoccupied with getting up the nerve to touch him to follow the plot. Every Saturday played out pretty much the same way.

First there was my pep talk: "OK, you can do this, just lean on his shoulder. On the count of three: one . . . two . . . oh, my God, I can't." I always wussed out.

Then, I just waited for him to make a move: "Kiss me. Kiiiiiisssss meeeeeee. Kiss me! . . . God, you idiot, you can't really be into the plot of *George of the Jungle*!"

Finally, he would lean over the armrest and start kissing me. Sometimes things would get really hot and heavy, and he'd pull me over on top of him. Then, it would just stop. And I'd be stranded: "Is he serious? Now what? I'm supposed to slink back to my seat like nothing happened? Or stay on his lap and twist my head around like I'm suddenly interested in the movie?"

When I first started dating, guys were a total mystery to me. I had no idea how to relate to them because I thought they didn't really care about girls. I was convinced that guys couldn't enjoy the emotional aspects of relationships—I thought they just wanted to hook up. And I assumed that guys were never nervous around girls because I believed that they had all the power in dating relationships.

It never occurred to me that maybe my boyfriend was every bit as freaked out as I was—and that's why it took him thirty minutes to finally kiss me. It hit me like a brick wall when I realized that: guys do have feelings, they do have insecurities, and they do like relationships.

The secret to feeling more confident around guys (if you're not already) is understanding that they're not that different from girls. Once you realize that guys are people, too, it's much easier to know how to act around them. And once you believe that they can be interested in you as a person, and not just you as a sex object, feeling confident around them comes more naturally. This chapter is all about guys and how they're not that different from girls—it's about their bodily hang-ups, their sexual concerns, and how they really feel about girls and relationships.

GIRLS' BODIES/GUYS' BODIES

The biggest tomboy in my sixth grade class got her first period when she was with a bunch of guys watching the Super Bowl. When she told a big group of girls about it at a birthday party, I'm sure it was one of the first times she related better to girls than she did to guys. She may have worn Dartmouth football jerseys, played basketball with the guys at lunch, and watched sports with them on the weekends, but that didn't change the fact that none of them could talk her through how to use a tampon.

At least at my school, puberty really had a way of splitting the guys and girls apart. It drove home the point that guys and girls were different because it drew our attention to our physical differences: our genitals. Because guys didn't have to deal with growing boobs or getting periods, my girlfriends and I started to resent them. Our bodies made us feel vulnerable and insecure, and it didn't seem like guys had to deal with those feelings at all. We thought that guys had it easy, and that made them intimidating.

I didn't know it when I was younger, but guys do feel confused, embarrassed, and inadequate because of their bodies. Although guys and girls obviously have different equipment, when it comes to the emotional issues that surround how our genitals look, smell, and behave, guys deal with the same sorts of feelings we do. These are some of the issues that guys have with their bodies.

Pitching tents. I think of boners as guys' unexpected visitors. Just as we have to worry about getting our periods unexpectedly and being embarrassed by blood on our clothes, guys have to worry about being embarrassed by an unexpected lump in their pants.

Imagine a guy getting a hard-on when he's dancing with a girl. How is he supposed to deal with it? He could stick his butt out really far to make sure the girl doesn't feel it, but that would look ridiculous. He could reach down his pants and try to adjust it, but then the girl might notice. He could proudly poke the girl with it and wink, but that would be really sleazy.

Guys worry about their bodies embarrassing them in front of girls in the same way that we worry about our bodies embarrassing us in front of guys. We don't want guys to get grossed out when they see one of our tampons, and guys don't want us to get grossed out because we see them with a boner. Guys are every bit as concerned with looking dumb in front of us as we are with looking dumb in front of them.

The size of the boat. Guys obsess about the size of their penis in the same way that a girl might fixate on the size of her boobs. Many guys see their penis as a symbol of their manhood and use it as a clear-cut physical way to compare themselves with other guys to see if they measure up. And thanks to the stereotype that penis size is a direct translation of how good a guy will be in bed, guys can feel really insecure about not being big enough or about other guys being bigger. Imagine the anxiety that a guy has the first time a girl sees it. Even if he's sittin' pretty at six inches (average is five and a half), there's always the chance that the last penis the girl saw was the size of a bull's.

Even though we tend to think of girls as being the ones who are more self-conscious about being naked, it's really guys who are risking more by taking off their clothes. When a guy gets naked, although you may already know roughly what his body will look like, when it comes to his penis, any size is possible. A guy has to wonder if you're going to look at his penis and think, "That's it?" And that must make him feel totally vulnerable.

The scent of a ball sack. Many guys will admit that their balls are the "one part of a dude's body that starts to smell minutes after he gets out of the shower." Some guys take lots of showers to deal with the odor. Others put powder on the area to try to soak up the sweat. And then there are those who feel like: "It's balls. They don't smell great. Who cares?" No matter how self-conscious a guy may or may not be about his ball odor, the fact remains that, just like vaginas, balls have a smell.

The point is, even though a guy's "privates" are clearly different from a girl's, he still has to deal with the same sorts of bodily concerns. Guys can be intimidating, but when you keep in mind that they're not always as confident as they may seem, it makes them more approachable. Guys don't have an overly easy time with their bodies, and they don't have an overly easy time dealing with sex either.

GUYS AND SEX

Many girls believe that only females have concerns about sex. We worry: "Will it hurt?" "Will I get pregnant?" "Is he worth it?" "Will he think I'm good?" Meanwhile, we assume that a guy's thought process is somewhere along the lines of: "Duuude—I'm gonna get laid."

But it's not that guys don't have concerns about sex; it's just that they're not always comfortable talking about them. In many social circles, if a guy expresses a sentiment other than "Hell, yeah!" with regard to sex, then his friends might call him a pansy or a pussy. Guys aren't encouraged to parade around the locker room talking about their sexual fears or inadequacies. A lot of guys feel pressure to come across as tough and confident, which isn't in line with, "Hey, guys—I'm a little concerned that I won't be able to perform."

The truth is, guys do have sexual concerns that go beyond how they can get themselves laid. Nearly all guys worry about their performance and about the possibility that their penises might make them look bad.

If guys spoke more openly about their sexual problems, you would hear about the following concerns.

Erectile Dysfunction

Even though young men may be in their "sexual prime," it's not uncommon for them to experience difficulty achieving or maintaining an erection. Although some failed erections are the result of drinking, doing drugs, or taking antidepressants, the majority of erectile problems are caused by anxiety. After all, guys have a lot of pressure resting on their penises. If a guy can't get hard, it can really take the steam out of a below-the-waist hookup—not to mention make intercourse impossible.

When a young man has problems getting it up, he can feel like a complete idiot or a sexual dud. He knows that he wants sex, but for some reason his body isn't responding, and he can't get an erection. He may react by feeling both pissed at himself and embarrassed about looking stupid in front of his partner. Some guys even get freaked out that their erectile "failure" means something about their ability to perform under pressure. And that concern can become a self-fulfilling prophecy (since the more nervous a guy is, the more difficult it is for him to get an erection).

If you're hooking up with a guy and he's having trouble getting an erection, it's not a situation you can ignore. But it's tough to know what to say to a guy who can't get hard. You can't exactly tell him: "Don't worry, baby, it looks cuter limp anyway."

Although there's no magic catchphrase that's going to make the guy feel 100 percent comfortable, there are things you can do for your partner that will make the situation less awkward. Express to him that you understand sometimes penises have a mind of their own. Say something like, "It's all right—I'd rather just cuddle tonight anyway." For guys to have an erection, they have to feel comfortable and confident. The more relaxed you make him feel about his erectile troubles, the easier it will be for him to get hard in the future. There are times that, for whatever reason, a guy just can't get hard, and that doesn't mean that he's impotent.

The most important thing to remember about a guy's erectile problems is that they are never your fault. They have *nothing* to do with how attracted a guy is to you. Erectile problems are caused by a guy's lack of confidence in his ability to "perform" (or by his use of alcohol, drugs, or medications). If a guy tries to blame you for his failed erection, it's because his ego is threatened. For an insecure guy, "You don't do it for me" is a better explanation than "I'm having trouble performing under pressure." If a guy is immature enough to try and cut you down to make himself feel better, it's a good thing that he couldn't get it up—because he's definitely not the kind of guy you want to be sleeping with.

Premature Ejaculation

Premature ejaculation (when a guy has an orgasm before he or his partner wants him to) is another sexual problem that guys worry about. You can imagine how embarrassing it is for a guy who's all psyched about having sex, and by the time it starts, it's over. Young guys can feel tremendous pressure to come across as sexually competent, and nothing screams "amateur" like coming too quickly.

The last thing that a guy wants is the reputation of a "minute man," but, realistically, most beginners aren't that far from the minute mark. It's likely that when you first start having sex, the guy you're having sex with may have some problems with coming too quickly. For a guy who doesn't have a lot of experience, the physical and emotional arousal of a sexual encounter can be too overwhelming to hold himself back. The best thing you can do for a guy who is having these types of difficulties is to let him know that it's OK and that it happens to everyone. As he gets more used to having sex, he'll be able to be more relaxed and last longer.

Whenever you confront any type of sexual malfunction with a guy, be supportive and let him know that it's no big deal. But if he starts acting like a jerk because he's embarrassed, make sure to call him on it. Tell him that it's not fair for him to be an ass to you because *he* feels inadequate. If a guy is putting you down because he didn't meet his own sexual expectations, it is his way of trying to save face. His sexual problems, whatever they may be, are always *his* problems—it's never OK for him to take those problems out on you.

GUYS WANT SEX

All technical problems aside, guys want to have sex. In fact, because they want sex so much, girls are often told that it's *all* that they want. But just because guys want to have sex, it doesn't mean that they don't want emotional intimacy as well. The need to be close to another person isn't a "girl need"—it's a human need. This is not to say that you won't encounter some guys who do just want to get laid; you probably will. Luckily, the majority of guys have needs that are more complex.

Although it's instinctive to look at a guy's desire for sex as something that's threatening, wanting sex doesn't make a guy an automatic jerk. Many girls assume that guys want to get laid only because they want to get off. But if this were really true, men would drop some cash on porn and a blow-up doll and be done with girls once and for all.

And yet, nearly every guy would agree that he would rather have sex with a girl than with his hand. So it can't just be the orgasm that attracts guys to sex. Men like sex because they like to be touched—all over their bodies, not just on their Johnsons.

For girls who believe that the penis is the axis around which men's worlds revolve, it can be hard to grasp the idea that men enjoy sex in part because they like being held. It's difficult to imagine that men opt for a hookup over masturbation because deep down, they just want to be spooned. Even Mr. Player Pimp seems a little less intimidating when you imagine him lying in bed with a little bubble over his head that says, "Hold me."

GUYS LIKE RELATIONSHIPS

Many girls are taught to see guys as sex-crazed machines that could never actually care about them. When a machine malfunctions and grows a heart, it can seem so unbelievable that you agree to be his girlfriend just because he's willing to be in a relationship. He may have been arrested twice, make straight Ds, and be a little ugly, but if he'll be your boyfriend, he almost seems like a good catch.

But the fact is, you don't have to settle *for* whatever guy is willing to settle *down*. Believe it or not, most guys like relationships (although, in all honesty, they may not even know that themselves). A lot of guys never get the chance to show their emotions or talk about their feelings. Being with a girl allows many guys to open up in ways they can't with their male friends. Even though we tend to think of guys as the ones who hate commitment, studies indicate that, on the whole, married men are happier than married women. Although it may not always be obvious, guys have emotional needs as well.

*"Not so **intimidating** now, huh?"*

From the Horse's Mouth
(Guys talk about sex, girls, and their bodies)

"A new girl will always make a guy nervous because you feel like you have to impress her. The way you dress, the way you smell, what you say . . . everything about you has to be perfect."—Nelson, 22

"I find it sexy when a girl wants to hold off on sex for a while because it shows she respects herself and the relationship enough to let it get to the right point."—Cory, 19

"When I was fifteen a girl told me, 'don't ever let a girl brush up against a boner. It's really gross!' For years I was nervous about having a noticeable erection."—Adam, 24

"I love being in relationships—having someone to share things with, someone to chill with, and someone to be there for you."—Justin, 20

"I decided to have sex for the first time when I felt comfortable with the girl I was with. It is definitely something that I will remember for the rest of my life."—Aaron, 22

"Guys do a lot of things to impress girls. We don't drive nice cars because we like nice cars, we don't care—we'd drive around in a piece of shit! We drive nice cars because girls like nice cars. It's all about the general consensus of what girls like."—Steve, 19

WE'RE THE SCARY ONES

Sometimes girls get so caught up in feeling intimidated by guys that it doesn't occur to us that the reverse may be true as well. Although it can seem like guys have all the power in relationships, many guys think that it's girls who have the control. Traditionally, guys are the ones who are supposed to ask girls out on dates—and that definitely makes the guy the vulnerable one. The guy has to get up the courage to say, "Wanna go out?" and face the possibility of a girl's flat-out rejection.

Some guys may seem cocky and completely confident, but usually the "I don't give a shit," tough-guy attitude is just the image they want to project. If guys really didn't care about what girls thought about them, would they be loud and obnoxious in class? Would they grab door frames and do pull-ups? Would they make big scenes in public places? Many of the "stupid" things guys do are attempts to get girls' attention or make girls laugh. Guys are just as confused about how to act around us as we are about how to act around them. They have no clue about what we're thinking and no insight into how we're feeling.

Anything that's unknown is scary and intimidating. So if you're freaked out by guys, keep in mind that they're not that different from you. If you're wondering how a guy feels in a certain situation, think about how you would feel if you were in his shoes. Although guys and girls may have been taught to express their feelings in different ways, much of what we actually feel is the same. The better you are able to see your relationship with a guy as a relationship with another human instead of with "a male," the easier it will be to relate to him.

Chapter 5:

Virginity
To Lose It?
Or Not to Lose It?

MY VIRGINITY

J had the loss of my virginity all planned out. I decided that I wanted all my best friends to be there with me when I lost it—for moral support. So I picked out an outfit that included all of them: a lacy bra one size too small that Leah gave me, a black thong that Anna left at my house a year before, and a necklace that Elizabeth wore every day in eighth grade (that somehow ended up in my jewelry box).

The timing was perfect. Spring, my senior year in high school, and my parents were out of town. I felt like hot stuff because I was going to have an exciting night even though it was a Tuesday.

I told the guy I was dating that I was finally ready to have sex. I thought having sex with him was a good move because it would mean that he could "start to really care about me." He wasn't as into me as I wanted him to be, and I figured that this would solve that problem.

When my boyfriend got to my house, he suggested that we take shots of tequila to make the process go more smoothly. We both took three with no chaser. But it takes a while for tequila to kick in, and I was still scared out of my mind. I made him dance with me to Aaron Neville to calm my nerves and stall the situation. A quarter of the way into track three, he picked me up over his shoulder and took me to my bedroom.

I was truly prepared for the situation. Tequila breath, a blue condom that someone had given me as a joke (and had sat in my glove compartment for a year), and a guy who had already had sex with seven—or was it eight?—other girls. (What really counts as sex?) He put on the condom. Great—I was about to lose it to a blue dick. He got on top of me, and I scrunched my eyes shut, waiting for what every other girl describes as excruciating pain.

"Shit!" he said.

"What?"

"I went limp."

"What?"

"I'm not hard anymore."

I had heard what he had said the first time, but *what?* Was he kidding me? Had I really finally made up my mind to have sex, picked out an outfit, gotten drunk—and on a Tuesday night, too—for this? It was as if someone had said that the prom had been canceled as I was slipping into my dress. This was my virginity, dammit, and Mr. Blue Dick was screwing it all up.

In Retrospect

As frustrating as it was not to have sex as I had planned, it was also kind of a relief, as if I had been pardoned on death row moments before my execution. I really wasn't ready to have sex the first time I tried. Now I think of the erectile problem we encountered as divine intervention. When I finally did have sex, it was under much better circumstances: it was for me and not for him; I left my friends out of the equation; I was sober; and (thankfully) the condom was a normal color and not a year old.

This chapter is about deciding if you *really* want to have sex and how to say no if you don't.

Common Misunderstandings about Sex

Making the decision to have sex is difficult because, as a virgin, there's no way to know what it will actually be like. Everyone who's had sex will tell you different things: some have amazing first experiences, and others' experiences are just awful. As a result of the mixed reviews, many girls develop misconceptions about what it's like to lose their virginity, how they will feel afterward, and how sex will change their relationships. Those misconceptions make it even harder to make the right decision. The following are five misunderstandings I had about sex and virginity as I was growing up.

You Will Lose Your Virginity As Planned

I always assumed that the first time you *tried* to have sex would be the first time you actually did it. If people can do a five-hundred-piece jigsaw puzzle in one night, how can you botch a puzzle with only two parts? You stick the peg in the hole. It doesn't seem that complicated.

Yet amazingly enough, it is complicated, and there's a lot that can go wrong the first time you have sex. Maybe he can't stay hard because he's too freaked out, or maybe it seems like no matter how much he pokes at your vagina, nothing is going to make its way in. If the first time you try to have sex fails, it can be very frustrating. Here you've gotten all mentally prepared to take the plunge, and then the mechanics of the whole thing mess up.

But even if the mechanics are going right, it doesn't mean that you *have* to have sex. Having *planned* on losing your virginity is not a document signed in your virginal blood that it will actually happen. Just because you thought that you were ready doesn't mean that you're obligated to do it if you change your mind. You can decide that you don't want to have sex at any time, even if it means backing out at the very last second. You never "owe" a guy sex because he thought it was going to happen, because you said it was going to happen, or because you've done everything but.

You may not lose your virginity exactly how and when you imagined you would, but that's OK. The important thing is that you're completely comfortable with the situation and that you're doing it safely, not that it happens on the exact night you thought it would. It's fine to have a game plan, as long as you accept that it may not play out as predicted. And while you're thinking about it, you might want to think up an *exit* plan as well—just in case you change your mind.

Losing Your Virginity Has to Be Physically Painful

Many girls (especially those who lost their virginity when they were younger) describe the experience as very physically painful. This is because the vagina, just like the penis, is very sensitive to your mental state. If you're a little freaked out, it will tighten up involuntarily. So maybe your head is saying, "I'm going to have sex," but your vagina is saying, "Yeah, right, buddy—no chance." If you're nervous, not only is your vagina tighter, but also it's harder to become sexually aroused, meaning that your vagina isn't very lubricated.

The combination of both a tight and unlubricated vagina can make sex painful. If you use a lubricated condom the first time you have sex, it will help some. But you may also want a tube of K-Y jelly or another water-based lubricant nearby. Your partner can spread the lubricant on the outside of the condom before you start having sex and reapply it whenever necessary.

The best thing you can do to make losing your virginity as comfortable as possible is to relax. Don't drop your panties and jump right into it; you and your partner should take some time to touch and kiss each other. You may want your partner to put a finger or two in you before he inserts his penis. (That way, you can get more used to the feeling of something inside of your vagina.) Most importantly, your partner should take his time. Losing your virginity shouldn't remind you of a construction worker jack-hammering a sidewalk; your partner should be slow and gentle.

Losing Your Virginity Has to Be Emotionally Painful

The way we talk about having sex for the first time sets us up for emotional disappointment. We talk about "losing our virginity" as though it will inevitably be something that we want back. It sounds more like a defeat than a celebration, so naturally, many girls worry about feeling "used," "dirty," or completely vulnerable after having sex. It's true that having sex in the wrong situation could make you feel that way, but if you're truly ready, most likely you won't.

Deciding that you're ready to have sex depends on many factors. First and foremost, you must feel comfortable and secure with the person you're about to have sex with. This means you can trust that your partner will give you the emotional support you need, both while you're having sex and after the act is over. It also means that if you need that emotional support, you won't be too shy to ask for it. Second, be sure that the reason you want to have sex is coming from inside of you (*you* want to share an intimate physical experience with someone), not outside of you (pressure from your friends or the guy). And last, sex should be something that you feel comfortable with on a physical, psychological, emotional, and spiritual level. In order for you to enjoy sex, you must be at ease with the act itself.

If you are comfortable with having sex, you're doing it because you want to, you trust your partner, and you're set to use protection, so losing your virginity should not be an upsetting experience. Having sex for the first time should be exciting. It's probably something you have thought about, talked about, and imagined for a long time; now you're

finally doing it. This is a time that you get to discover new things about yourself, your body, and your sexuality. And that is empowering.

If you do find yourself regretting having sex, remember that you will have many chances to make up for a crappy first time or a crappy boyfriend. Although you may have made a bad decision, you can always learn from the ways you screwed up in the past and know how to avoid making the same mistakes in the future. A few bad decisions about sex don't have to set you up for a lifetime of irresponsible sexual choices or ungratifying sexual experiences.

Sex Will Create Feelings That Aren't Already There

Before you have sex for the first time, you may overestimate the bond it will create. A guy may say that he can't really care about you unless you have sex with him, or that he needs sex to stay in the relationship. And since you don't know what sex is like, it's hard to know whether or not to believe him.

When you're a virgin, sex can seem like a mysterious act that's too intense for words. But when you finally do have sex, many people react with, "That's it? Did I really spend five hours on the phone with my best friend contemplating whether or not to do *that*?" We build up the idea of sex so much that it's natural to feel slightly disillusioned after the five-minute romp that ends many people's virginities. Don't get me wrong— sex is a big deal, just not always in the way you might expect.

Having sex will not make a guy who isn't in love with you fall in love with you, or create feelings that aren't already there. It can make you feel more vulnerable or slightly closer to someone, but it is not going to alter the course of your relationship or completely change your outlook on life. If a guy cares about you, he will care about you whether or not you have sex with him. If he doesn't want to be in a relationship with you, sex is not going to change that.

Sex Is Like Potato Chips: Once You Pop, You Just Can't Stop

I was always afraid that once I started having sex, it would mean that I had some sort of obligation to sleep with every other guy I dated. As if after losing it I would automatically have to screw any old schmuck that asked me to bed. Having the justification of being a virgin was my safety-net reason for not going to bed with someone. Without being able to hide behind my virginity as an excuse, I would have to find the courage to say, "I'm OK with the idea of having sex—I'm just not OK with the idea of having sex with *you*."

Although it may be easier to turn down sex if you're a virgin, not being one doesn't mean you can't or shouldn't say no. Every time you decide to have sex with someone new, you should base the decision on how you feel about that person and your relationship with him, not on how many other people you have slept with. ("I've already had sex with four guys, why not make it five?") Deciding to have sex with someone is a big decision, which is something that many of us think about our first time, then may forget with the next few. But after putting number one through a lengthy screening process, why should number two get to waltz right in just because someone else happened to get there first? If you spent a lot of time deliberating whom to lose your virginity to, it's backwards to let the next guy you sleep with be Joe Blow.

DEALING WITH THE PRESSURE TO HAVE SEX

There can be a significant amount of pressure to have sex. Maybe most of your friends have had sex, and you don't want to feel left out. Or maybe you're dating someone who continues to proposition you, even though you always say no. Whatever the pressure may be, having sex because of other people (be it your friends or a guy) will never lead to enjoyable experiences.

If some of your friends have already had sex, you might feel like you should do it too. This pressure may come directly from a friend; sometimes if a girl isn't totally comfortable with the fact that she had sex, she'll try to persuade her friends to do it to make herself feel better about her own decision. It's kind of like the "I don't want to walk into that party alone" mentality—except for in this case "that party" is being sexually active. If you have a friend who keeps nagging you about being a virgin, know that, if she were secure with herself, she wouldn't be so concerned about whether or not *you* had sex.

Being one of the few virgins in your group of friends can feel like being the girl who always doesn't get the joke. When all your friends are talking about sex, maybe you feel like you have to shut up because you haven't done it yet. If you find yourself feeling left out because you're a virgin, the best way to feel "more educated" is to go to a library or bookstore and spend a few hours skimming through sex books. Then, next time the topic of sex comes up, you can talk about some position you read about, what condom you heard was the best, or any other juicy tidbit you can remember. You can have way more to say about sex after researching it than by doing it once or twice with a guy who probably doesn't know what he's doing. Having sex "just to be able to talk about it" won't actually give you much fuel for conversation.

Most likely, if you're feeling pressured to have sex, it's not coming from your friends—it's coming from a guy. Telling a guy that you don't want to have sex with him can take a lot of guts. It's hard to say no if things get to the point where he's on top of you naked, has just pulled out a condom, and is asking, "Are we going to do this or not?" Many girls in this situation feel like they can't say no because they're almost doing it already. But it's never too late to say no to sex.

No matter how a guy phrases "Do you want to have sex," he is asking you a question, not making a demand. It's not a command that's disguised as a question, like "Do you want to pass me the salt?" It's an inquiry that requires some deliberation. And after thinking about it, if you decide the answer is no, then you should tell him no.

If you are propositioned in the heat of the moment and don't want to have sex, you can say something as simple as "I'm not ready to have sex," "I don't want to have sex with you," or even just "No." If a guy is continually pestering you, make it clear that you will tell him whether you want to have sex and that he doesn't have to keep asking. You are never required to have sex with a guy—even if you're in bed with him naked, even if he's not a virgin, and even if for some reason he assumed that the two of you were going to sleep together. If a guy actually cares about you, he is going to stay interested whether or not you sleep with him.

Girls' Reflections on Virginity

"I waited twenty-one years to lose my virginity, and, when I finally did, it was to someone I wasn't very close to. If I had the opportunity to do it differently, I would. But at the same time, I find no use in having regrets, and I learned things about myself which have led to other more fulfilling experiences that I would never take back."—Leah, 21

"When I lost my virginity, I was sixteen. I was one of the first out of my group of friends, so I was hesitant to tell people because I didn't want them to think I was bragging."—Megan, 21

"I was twelve when I lost it, and, thinking back on it, I wish I had waited until I was older. It made me grow up a little too fast." —Emily, 23

"The first time I tried to have sex it didn't work."—Mom, 56 (Thanks for the info!)

"I was comfortable with being a virgin, despite the fact that some of my friends weren't. I waited until I was ready and trusted the person. I don't regret doing it at all."—Jess, 21

"The title of virgin is so annoying. It puts so much pressure on the first time. It's like everyone who hasn't had intercourse is in the same category as everyone who hasn't ever even kissed someone, and then you have sex once, and boom, you get bumped into a completely different category."—Lauren, 21

"For me, losing my virginity was a much bigger deal emotionally than it was physically. Physically it's not much different than any other sex act, but emotionally it carries a whole new set of fears and responsibilities."—Alison, 21

"I was in college before I lost my virginity, and sometimes I felt like other people there thought that I wasn't open to trying new things just because I was a virgin. I was into trying new things—it's just that I hadn't found someone I was comfortable trying them with."—Cailin, 22

THE BOTTOM LINE: SHOULD I DO IT OR NOT?

You may spend months agonizing over the decision to have sex. And though you may get loads of advice from other people, it's a decision that eventually you have to make on your own. If you're in the process of making this decision, you may find these next lists helpful. As you read through them, keep in mind that even if all signs point to yes, it doesn't necessarily mean that you should have sex. Only you (and not a friend's advice, a magazine article, or this book) can figure that out for sure.

Signs Sex Is a Bad Idea

I'm about to have sex because I don't want to be "sexually inexperienced." Some girls feel pressured to have sex because they don't want other people to think that they're inexperienced. But just 'cause you picked up a guitar once and played around with the strings, it doesn't make you any more of a rock star than if you never touched it at all. Having sex once or twice doesn't make someone a "sexpert."

I'm about to have sex because I can't go to college as a virgin. Some girls think that college is a place where there's lots of casual sex, and they figure they'd rather lose their virginity to someone they know from high school than some random frat boy in college. Others think that, once you're in college, you're just expected to have sex, so they should get their first time "out of the way" before they get there. But not everyone in college has had sex, and not every relationship in college includes sexual intercourse. Many girls go off to college a virgin. According to the Alan Guttmacher Institute—a nonprofit organization that conducts sex research—only 60 percent of girls have had sex by the time they are eighteen.

I'm about to have sex, and I only have one condom (and it may or may not be blue). There are many things that can go wrong the first time (or any time) you try to have sex: maybe the condom breaks, or maybe you put it on, and then he loses his erection. It's always best to have some backups on hand so that you won't even be tempted to have sex without one.

I'm about to have sex because I want a guy to care more about me. Having sex will not make someone care about you any more than he already does. When you are making the decision to have sex, be sure that "I want him to be happy with me" or "I don't want him to dump me" aren't factors in your decision.

I'm about to have sex, and I'm too scared to even use a tampon. If you're not comfortable with the idea of sticking things inside you, you should reconsider your decision to have sex. In order to enjoy sex, you have to be comfortable with your vagina—if you're not, you're not ready. Besides, there are other ways to be physically intimate with someone that don't include intercourse (see p. 79).

I'm having sex to prove I'm attractive. Sex should not be used as proof that you are sexually desirable. Having sex so that you feel wanted will just leave you feeling used and dirty (which isn't going to make you feel more good looking). Feeling more confident in yourself and your appearance is not something you will get as a result of having sex.

I'm about to have sex, and I'm wasted. You definitely shouldn't make the decision to have sex for the first time (or any time) while you're drunk or stoned. Every girl I have known who has done this regrets her decision. Losing your virginity while drunk is a bad idea, even if you made up your mind to do it while you were sober. Your virginity is probably an experience that you have thought about for a long time, so it sucks if your memory of it is a blur. It's like having front-row seats to your favorite band and then going to the concert messed up and not remembering anything about it. (And, aside from that, no decent guy should have sex with you when you aren't thinking clearly.)

You *Might* be Ready for Sex If . . .

I'm comfortable with the relationship I have with the guy I may lose it to. For some, this means someone who says he loves you, and for others it means someone who says he knows your last name. Many people desire a certain amount of trust and intimacy with the first person they are going to sleep with. As long as you have that *before* you have sex (and this doesn't mean anticipating it to come after), your first experience can be a fulfilling one.

I know that the person I am about to have sex with cares about me. The first time that you have sex, it should be with someone who will look out for you, not just some jerk who's going to get on top of you and be like,

"Yeah, buddy, I'm gettin' laid!" The guy you lose your virginity to should be someone who will go slowly and keep checking in to make sure that you're OK.

I don't feel any pressure to have sex. You may face a lot of pressure to have sex, whether it's from the friend who calls you "Virgin Mary," some guy who calls you a "prude," or your boyfriend, who says he'll break up with you if you don't have sex with him. Ultimately, you should have sex because *you* want to, not because someone else thinks that you should.

I'm comfortable with the idea of having sex. For some people, having sex before marriage means going against their religious beliefs or moral values. Make sure that you are morally and spiritually at peace with the idea of having sex before you do it. And, more basically, be sure that the physical act doesn't still seem "gross" or scary.

I'm going to try my best not to get pregnant or get nasty genital sores. Don't be half-assed about birth control and safer sex. Having sex means taking risks; you should know all the risks you are facing and take precautions against them before you have sex. If you're safer about it, sex is much less stressful and much more fun. (For more information about sexually transmitted diseases and safer sex, see "Sexually Transmitted Diseases," p. 87, and "Contraception and Protection," p. 109.)

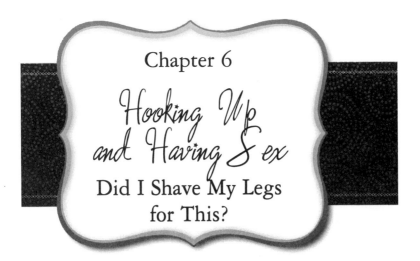

Chapter 6

Hooking Up and Having Sex

Did I Shave My Legs for This?

he first time I had an orgasm with another person was by dry humping. I didn't even let the guy know that I had one because I felt embarrassed about it; it just didn't seem normal to get off that way. At the time, I had no idea that dry humping had a name, let alone that it was something many couples did and enjoyed. I assumed I was a weirdo because I liked being rubbed up against while fully clothed, more than actually being fingered. When it came to my first sexual experiences, I was half-shocked, half-disturbed, and completely confused.

Early sexual experiences often feel weird because you're doing something that you haven't done before or haven't done that much. When things progress from making out to sex acts that involve genitals, it can take some getting used to. This chapter is about feeling more comfortable with all sex acts—everything from fingering to fornication, and seeing past sex myths that are total BS.

SEX MYTHS

Because hooking up is something that most girls figure out as they go along, many look back on aspects of their sexual past and think, "Why did I do that?" Many girls believe that, when it comes to sex, there are things they "have to do," things they "should do," and things they "may as well do." And as a result, they get roped into sex acts that they don't *really* want to be engaging in. The following are five BS sex myths that should never influence your decision to do something sexual.

Myth #1: You Must Reciprocate

No matter how many times we've heard and accepted the phrase "life's not fair," there's often pressure to keep things "fair and even" with regard to sex. Many girls think that, if a guy attempts to please them sexually, they *have* to return the favor. But there's no need to keep a sexual score-card. Just because he may be quick to touch your genitals, it doesn't mean that you have to jump at your first opportunity to touch his. It's not a cardinal hookup sin not to reciprocate.

When a guy does something to pleasure you, he should be doing it because he wants to make you feel good, not because he wants you to get him off afterward. If he is only pleasuring you to make you feel obligated to pleasure him, then he's sleazy, manipulative, and doesn't deserve a "sexual favor." You never "owe" a guy an orgasm, so if you aren't comfortable touching his penis, then don't do it. If not having an even "scorecard" is going to make you feel uneasy, then don't let him do anything to you in the first place.

Myth #2: Never, Ever Give Him Blue Balls

One of the ways that a girl can get pressured into "returning the favor" is by a guy telling her that he will have extremely achy "blue balls" if he doesn't have an orgasm. The way some guys talk about blue balls, you would think that if a guy doesn't get off after he gets turned on, his balls would actually turn blue and fall off. (They don't really—they just get a little achy.) In reality, most of the hype that surrounds blue balls is melodramatic BS. Although the painful sensation of "blue balls" does happen, it doesn't happen as often as some guys would like you to believe.

Blue balls occur only when a man is *about to have an orgasm,* then for whatever reason doesn't. If a guy has an erection that is not "taken care of," it will not cause blue balls. Hooking up with a guy—even if he gives you digital (hand/finger) or oral sex—and then not getting him off will not cause it. And, most of the time, even ending sexual intercourse before a guy has had an orgasm will not cause it either.

Worse-case scenario, if a guy does get blue balls, all he has to do is jack off, and the pain goes away. The moral of the story is that it's a waste of energy to be concerned about a problem when the solution lies right in the palms of the guy's hands. Never let the threat of blue balls con you into touching a guy's penis if you don't want to. Even if he *is* going to get blue balls, you don't need to "relieve" him if you're not comfortable doing it. He is perfectly capable of reaching an orgasm by himself if he really feels that it's necessary.

Myth #3: Sex Acts Are a Good Way to Get Attention from Guys

Some girls think that a good way to keep guys from ignoring them is to "put out" and give guys sexual pleasure. While it may be true that giving guys sexual favors will make them pay attention to you, that doesn't mean that you should do it. Guys would also notice you if you got naked and streaked down the halls of your school, but that doesn't make it a good idea. Not all attention is good attention.

Wanting attention from guys usually boils down to wanting guys to like you, but there is a difference between attention and liking. Although hooking up with a lot of guys may make them temporarily interested in you, it won't last any longer than the sexual encounter, and it won't make them like you any more than they did before you hooked up. If you want guys to like you, they first have to respect you. And they aren't going to respect you if they think they can use you for sex because they'll think that you're not respecting yourself.

You should never feel that being able to please a guy sexually is all you have to offer. Every girl has traits that the right guy will find appealing. But getting other people to notice them often starts with having the confidence to notice them yourself. Confidence is tricky because there's no easy way to feel it, and it may fluctuate from day to day. The best way to build confidence is to concentrate on the permanent things you like about yourself that don't fluctuate. Focus on your sense of humor, your intelligence, your ability to be a great friend, or a special talent. Feeling good about yourself is something that has to come from the inside, not from a guy. The temporary boost you may feel from having a guy hang around because he thinks you're "easy" is only going to make you feel crappy in the long run.

Myth #4: Only Intercourse Really Matters

When we categorize sex acts in our mind, we tend to break them up into two groups: the ones you can do and still be a virgin and the one that makes you a nonvirgin. Because blow jobs, hand jobs, being fingered, or having someone go down on you don't count as losing your "virginity," it's easy to think that those activities don't count as sex. But just because a sex act doesn't affect your status as a "virgin," that doesn't mean it's not a big deal emotionally or physically, or that it doesn't really matter.

The first time that you engage in digital or oral sex can be every bit as overwhelming as the first time you have intercourse. But since most people don't make as big of a deal over their first digital and oral sexual experiences, some girls jump into them on a whim because "Whatever— it's not like it's sex." But these sex acts *are* sex. And engaging in any sex act before you're ready can make you feel just as uncomfortable as having intercourse before you're ready.

I like to think of sexual acts as a continuum rather than two separate categories. To me, the step between finger sex and oral sex is not that much smaller than the step between oral sex and intercourse. All sex acts are "important" enough to be thought about carefully before engaging in them, and in that way, intercourse shouldn't be put into a league of its own. Sure, only intercourse affects your status as a virgin, but that doesn't make it a good idea to go around giving out blow jobs like handshakes. Before you do anything sexual, no matter how big or small you might think the act, it's always a good idea to check with yourself and make sure that it's really what you want to be doing.

Myth #5: After You've Messed Up Once, It Doesn't Matter

Some girls think that, if they've had unprotected sex with a guy once, then there's no need to use a condom with him in the future. They figure, "If he has a sexually transmitted disease [STD], I probably already have it, so why bother?" But having unprotected sex with a guy does not ensure that you will contract any STD he may be carrying. Each time you have unprotected sex with *the same guy*, there is *a new risk* of contracting an STD. And the more you have sex without a condom, the more likely it will be that you catch something. So even if you haven't always used protection, it's never too late to start.

THE ACTS OF SEX

The first time I touched a penis, I literally just touched it. I thought that maybe I was ready to go a little further than just kissing, but at the last second I wussed out, ended up just poking it, and then quickly pulled my hand away. I called my best guy friend right afterward and started screaming, "Oh, my God, I touched it, I touched it!" To this day, my friend still makes fun of me for being so shocked and excited that I had actually dared to put my finger on a real live penis.

It's hard to know what to expect when your hookups move from just kissing into more sexual territory. Your first experiences with a penis can be very confusing and leave you feeling a bit uneasy. And the first time a guy goes near your vagina can be totally startling (for both you and the guy). One thing you can do that will definitely help make your experiences more enjoyable is to make sure that you are truly comfortable with what's going on. This may mean that you want things to happen gradually, by slowly getting used to the idea of "genital fondling," and not skipping straight into oral sex or intercourse. The following sections are briefings about what to expect as you progress from making out to sex.

Dry Humping

Dry humping is undoubtedly the most unappealing name for a sexual act. It sounds like something a lap dog does to your lounge chair, not something you want your boyfriend to do to you. But almost everyone dry humps eventually because, as gross as it sounds, it does feel good.

Yet as often as dry humping may occur, it's rarely discussed. Most girls don't tell their partner that he's a good dry humper or explain to their friends that they dry humped in the back of some guy's car for an hour. It feels a little awkward to participate in, or talk about, a sex act that involves keeping your clothes on.

As odd as it may seem, and as gross as it may sound, dry humping is a good way for you to pretend that you're having sex without actually doing it—like the simulation training that pilots complete before they're ready for the real thing. There's no reason to feel strange about dry humping because many couples do it when they are making out. And safety wise, it's the best sex act you can engage in (i.e., you can't get pregnant or an STD from rubbing against your partner with your clothes on).

Hands-On Experiences

The first time that many people come into contact with someone else's genitals is by touching them with their hands. Since these experiences tend to be your earliest, they also tend to be the most awkward. But as out of place as your hands may initially feel on your partner's genitals, it's a good starting point. Digital sex is often less stressful than oral sex or intercourse because you don't have to worry about getting an STD. And not having intercourse means that you don't have to worry about pregnancy. (Just make sure that he doesn't ejaculate near your vagina.) So if you're ready for the world of genital touching, hand jobs and being fingered are good places to begin.

Hand Jobs

Many girls I know find hand jobs awkward and scary. They worry about accidentally grabbing a guy's pubic hair or chafing his delicate skin. And some wonder why they should do something to a guy that he could do on his own. But despite the potential problems that a hand job may bring up, it's a very safe way to bring an orgasm into a sexual encounter.

If you're worried about chafing a guy, use a lubricant (lotion or baby oil works well) and, when you initially grab his penis, don't do it at the bottom (the part closest to his body), where you might get a fistful of hair. Keep in mind that he'll be so thrilled you're touching his penis that you'll be the only one worried about technique. As for the "he could do this on his own" argument, I'm sure all guys will tell you that a hand job is always better from someone else.

Getting Fingered

If you find being fingered to be slightly unpleasant, you're not an asexual freak with a dysfunctional vagina—you're one of many girls who are just having bad experiences. There are a few reasons that you may not enjoy being fingered. The first is that, when you're tense, your vagina tightens up. If a guy keeps trying to put his fingers in you, it might be a little unpleasant or even painful. The more you can relax, the better it will feel.

Second, some guys get so excited to have one finger in you that they want to put in more and more—like that camp game Chubby Bunny, when you try to see how many marshmallows you can fit into your mouth. Some guys don't understand how delicate they have to be with vaginas. Not only may they try to stick too much up there, but they may also have sharp nails or try to move in and out too quickly.

And last, clitoris, clitoris, clitoris. Many girls enjoy clitoral stimulation more than vaginal penetration. But since many guys (and girls) don't always know this, "fingering" is generally interpreted as sticking a finger (or three) into the vaginal hole, as opposed to rubbing a girl's clitoris, which is probably more pleasurable. (For more information about sexual pleasure, see "Pleasing Yourself," p. 43.)

If a guy is trying to please you the wrong way, you need to tell him. There is nothing wrong with saying, "Slow down"; "A little gentler, please"; or "No more fingers." And if you would rather have him rub your clitoris, tell him where it is, or put your hand over his and show him what to do. Most important, if he is hurting you, never hesitate to say, "Stop. That hurts." You should never endure a painful sexual encounter because you're afraid of giving a guy criticism. The reason he's fingering you in the first place is because it's supposed to feel good.

THE LAND DOWN UNDER

We tend to think of intercourse as the ultimate sex act, the one that really counts. But many people find oral sex more intimate and even more fulfilling. Close face-to-genital contact requires a huge amount of trust, and many people (especially women) find oral sex to be more pleasurable than intercourse.

Some girls choose to have oral sex as a way to avoid having vaginal sex. But it's important to know that having oral sex still puts you at risk for contracting sexually transmitted diseases. Your risk of contracting HIV and other STDs through oral sex is significantly lower than your risk of contracting it through intercourse. However, unprotected oral sex does still put you at *some* risk. To help protect yourself, you should use a condom when you go down on a guy and an oral dam when a guy goes down you. (For more information about sexually transmitted diseases and safer sex, see "Sexually Transmitted Diseases," p. 87, and "Contraception and Protection," p. 109.)

When Someone Goes Down on You

In order to fully enjoy the pleasures of oral sex, you have to be comfortable with the idea of your partner's face being *very* close to your vagina. This can be alarming because most women worry about the smell and taste of their genitalia: "Does my vagina smell bad?" "Does it taste bad?" "Is he going to be totally turned off after doing this to me?" With thoughts like that, there's no chance that you will enjoy yourself.

In truth, yes, your vagina has a smell, and it also has a taste. And so does every other vagina in the world; it comes with the territory. But the majority of guys are not misled about what they're getting themselves into when they get themselves into vaginas. I mean, you don't walk into a sushi restaurant expecting a meatball sub, and when your partner goes down on you, he's not expecting flowers. Besides, many men (especially as they get older) are turned on by the smell and taste of a healthy vagina.

As long as you shower regularly and don't have an infection, the smell of your vagina is normal, and you shouldn't worry about it. If the guy you are with doesn't like it, then he wouldn't offer to go down on you. As a last resort, if you're still insecure about the whole smell thing, the next time you go down on him, just give his balls a good whiff.

Note: The safest way to receive oral sex is to use an oral dam—a sheet of latex between your vagina and your partner's mouth. (For more information, see "Oral Dams," p. 116.)

Going Down on Him

The biggest blow-job issue for most girls is making the decision to spit or to swallow. Many of the reasons that girls cite for choosing either one are based on myths about semen. The following are a few faulty justifications that girls use to explain their blow-job policy.

"I spit because of the calories." I remember there was a rumor going around my high school that a typical load of semen contained as many calories as a Whopper. If a typical load of semen really had 610 calories, fruit-flavored ejaculate would be marketed to football players as a way to bulk up. In reality, it only contains about five.

"I swallow because I don't want the guy I'm going down on to feel rejected." This argument is a little ridiculous. The guy just got a blow job. If he feels rejected because you didn't swallow his semen (or let him ejaculate in your mouth), then he's either too insecure to be in a healthy sexual relationship, or he's too much of a jerk to deserve oral sex.

"I spit because I don't want to get an STD." Unfortunately, you cannot spit out an STD. Once you have performed unprotected oral sex on a guy, the damage is done. The only truly safe way to give a blow job is by using a condom—and that way you don't have to worry about spitting or swallowing at all. So instead of debating whether you want to spit or swallow, pick up a pack of flavored condoms and decide whether you want grape or cherry. No matter what flavor you choose, it will taste better (not to mention be safer) than if you don't use one.

AND FINALLY—SEX, SEX!

When most people think "sex," they think of sexual intercourse. Many people believe that intercourse is "real sex," that it's the be-all, end-all, and most intimate sex act you can share with another person. Much of this feeling stems from the fact that sexual intercourse involves so many risks. It is the easiest way to get an STD (aside from anal sex); it involves the risk of getting pregnant; and it's the sex act that most people consider to carry the most emotional hazards.

Intercourse is also the form of sex that is most romanticized and hyped up in the media. Largely because of the images in TV and movies, when most people conjure up images of sex, they envision romantic kissing, passionate thrusting, and sexy moaning. Many don't realize that when they actually have sex, they're going to have to deal with the not-so-desirable aspects that are just as much a part of many sexual encounters. As a result, many feel that their sex life is a failure if it doesn't meet up to their picture-perfect visions.

This Is What We See When We See Sex

In movies, we see hot, passionate sex where couples go at it on every surface in a house. We see lovers move seamlessly from the kitchen table to the bathroom counter without stumbling over furniture or awkwardly chasing each other around the house while naked. We see "perfect sex" where the couple doesn't have flushed faces or funky hair; they look fashionably disheveled. They don't grunt, squeal, or say something dumb in the heat of the moment; they passionately moan. The woman doesn't complain about not being able to have an orgasm because she just had three.

But this is not the kind of sex you will have (especially at the beginning), and it's not the kind of sex your friends are having either (although some may talk as though they are). Because this is the kind of sex shown in movies, you may assume that's how most couples' sex lives are and how yours should be. Having these types of expectations may make you feel unnecessarily excited to start having sex if you're a virgin. ("Damn, I can't wait to do that!") And if you've had sex, these images can make you feel completely sexually inadequate. ("The sex I'm having must really suck!") But what you see on TV and in movies is not what *anyone's* sex life looks like 99 percent of the time.

This Is What We Get When We Get Sex

When sex happens in real life, it usually looks nothing like what we see in the media. For one thing, it's not seamless. You're kissing, then you have to stop and lay down. (You don't fall gracefully lip-locked onto the bed.) You're heavily making out, then you have to tug at your shirt to get it off. (Your clothes don't always come off easily.) And when you've put on the condom and are finally all ready, you have to take the time to deliberately guide the guy's penis into your vagina—a process that can

"Not quite as hot as in the movies"

take from a few seconds to a few minutes (it usually doesn't slide in effortlessly). For sex scenes that aren't choreographed, the action isn't nonstop; there's much more fumbling around.

Real sex can be *really* awkward—like getting a mouthful of hair when you try to nibble on a guy's ear, or having your teeth clink when you try to kiss. Two sweaty bodies can make noises that sound a lot like farts, and that's not too sexy. And even if nothing happens that wasn't supposed to, the act of sex is messy (because of the bodily fluids), sweaty, and at times uncomfortable. The bottom line is that, much of the time, sex isn't really that sexy at all. But that's why it's so intimate and makes people feel vulnerable—because they're sharing the embarrassing moments as well as the "sexy" ones.

Sex *can* be amazing. But it isn't a lot of the time. The closer you are with your partner, and the more relaxed you can feel with him, the better your sex will be—because you'll feel secure enough to really get into it. You should think carefully about who you have sex with, not only because of your health, but also because it's only most enjoyable if it's with someone who makes you feel comfortable and it's something that *you* really want to do.

Chapter 7

Sexually Transmitted Diseases

Feel the Burn

A month after I lost my virginity, I was at the doctor's office for a regular checkup and happened to mention that I had a sore spot in my vagina.

"OK," my doctor said. "I'll just go ahead and test you for gonorrhea." He nonchalantly scribbled something on his clipboard and walked out, leaving me alone with a year-old *Newsweek* and my completely overactive imagination.

Oh, my God, gonorrhea? Gonorrhea?! (I knew absolutely nothing about it, but I figured if it rhymed with *diarrhea*, it had to be bad.) *I can't believe the doctor thinks I have an STD. How did this happen? Will people who find out be totally disgusted and afraid to touch me? Am I going to be that nasty girl that no one wants to share drinks with? The dirty one with gonorrhea? I'll never be able to have sex again. This isn't fair!*

As it turned out, I didn't have gonorrhea (although I did have a nuclear meltdown in front of a doctor and two nurses). But even if I had it, I could have been cured with antibiotics (something I wasn't aware of when I was sobbing about my life being over).

When I started having sex, the only thing I knew about STDs was that you didn't want them. I didn't know that some were curable and others weren't, or that even the curable ones could make you infertile. I thought that "I've been tested and I'm fine" was a green light to have sex with someone without a condom. And I assumed that only girls who slept around had to think about STD stuff.

WHY TO READ ON

It may be tempting to skip over this section because STDs are a major downer, and it's hard to believe that they could affect you. Maybe you only hook up with only good-looking guys who take showers and wear cologne. (They're so well dressed that they couldn't possibly have an STD!) Or maybe you go to a private school, or one of your parents is a doctor. (You're too smart to ever get an STD!) Or maybe you are sleeping with the captain of the basketball team who is a dead ringer for Jake Gyllenhaal. (He is way too cute to have an STD!) The problem is, as clean as he looks, as smart as you are, and as hot as he is, STDs can happen to *anyone*!

Because over half of all people will have some sort of STD in their lifetimes, STDs are something you want to know about. And because you can get many STDs through oral sex, they're something you want to know about even if you aren't planning on having intercourse anytime soon. By learning about the signs and symptoms of STDs, you can better recognize them in a partner and better recognize them in yourself. Since some STDs are harmless if caught early, you can avoid permanent damage to your reproductive system by treating them right away (something you can do only if you know what to look for and get regular checkups). This chapter is about STDs, how to protect yourself from them, and what you should know about being "tested."

ABSTINENCE AND MONOGAMY

The best way to protect yourself from STDs is to remain abstinent—in short, not have any kind of sex. Remaining abstinent can be very challenging, especially if many of your friends are sexually active. Even if you plan on being abstinent, you should learn about how to have safer sex just in case your plans fall through. Because things that you don't plan can happen anyway, it's best to be prepared for all possibilities.

If you are going to have sex, it is safest to do it within a long-term monogamous relationship (where both you and your partner are having sex only with each other). If you are having sex with only one person, and that person is having sex with only you, it greatly limits your exposure to STDs. The more people you have sex with, the more likely it is that you will get an STD. Although there is always a risk of contracting an STD when you're having sex, your risk is much lower if you have one partner for an extended period of time—and that partner is remaining faithful to you.

SEXUAL RISKS MADE EASY

Sexual Activity	STDs You Could Get		
Making Out	Mouth Herpes (potentially contagious all of the time, but most contagious if there is an open sore)		
Hand Job/ Getting Fingered	None		
Oral Sex	Genital Herpes Gonorrhea	Hepatitis B* HIV	Syphilis
Sexual Intercourse	Chlamydia Genital Herpes Gonorrhea	Hepatitis B* HIV HPV/Genital Warts	Syphilis
Anal Sex	Genital Herpes Gonorrhea Hepatitis B*	HIV HPV/Genital Warts Syphilis	
*If you are not vaccinated			

For quick reference, here's a list of which STDs you can get from different sexual activities. If you use a condom (or an oral dam for oral sex), your risk of catching these goes way down. But even condoms and oral dams don't make a sexual activity 100 percent safe.

Gonorrhea

Signs a guy is experiencing symptoms of this STD: "Dude! Check out this pus-like white stuff dripping out of my schlong . . . maybe that's why it burns and itches when I pee!"

Signs you may have this STD: "I haven't noticed anything weird down there, so I'm sure I'm fine."

Gonorrhea statistics: In the United States, gonorrheal infections are the most common in girls between the ages of fifteen to nineteen. Gonorrhea is also the second-most commonly reported bacterial STD.

Symptoms in men (should they occur): Although some guys can be infected with gonorrhea and not have any symptoms, the majority of them will have noticeable signs of infection. The symptoms usually take between two to five days to develop but can take as long as a month. When a guy has gonorrhea, he may experience pain when he is peeing or have sore or swollen testicles. Another common symptom is a creamy whitish, yellowish, or greenish liquid (not semen) dripping out of his penis. This is why some people call gonorrhea "the drip."

Symptoms in women (should they occur): When women are infected with gonorrhea, the majority of them have no symptoms at all. Those who do may not even notice them because they are so mild. If women do notice symptoms when infected with gonorrhea, they usually develop within ten days. These symptoms could include pain when peeing or having sex, bleeding in between periods, or a sore or swollen vagina.

Nongenital symptoms: Men and women can get gonorrhea in their throat or anus. People who are infected with gonorrhea of the throat often don't have any symptoms; when they do, they experience a sore throat. Most people who have anal gonorrhea also have no symptoms. The few that do may experience anal itching or pain when they go number two.

Treatment: If you are diagnosed with gonorrhea, there is no need to panic; it can be treated with antibiotics. (If multiple organs are infected, antibiotics will cure all of them.) The thing to freak out about is having an infection that is not diagnosed and is left untreated.

Why it can really suck: If gonorrhea is left untreated, the infection may spread to other organs and eventually cause pelvic inflammatory disease (PID), a serious condition that can cause permanent pelvic pain, infertility, and pregnancy complications. PID's symptoms can include pain in your lower stomach or back, pain during sex, feeling nauseous, having a fever, and bleeding in between periods. Having gonorrhea also puts you at a greater risk for contracting HIV if you are exposed.

How it is transmitted: You can get gonorrhea by having unprotected sex or oral sex with someone who is infected. In very rare cases, you can also get it by having infected fluids (semen, vaginal secretions, or saliva) come into contact with your genitals, anus, or throat (although you cannot get gonorrhea by kissing someone).

How to reduce your risk while still getting it on: To avoid getting gonorrhea, use a condom every time you have vaginal intercourse or anal intercourse, and use a condom or an oral dam every time you have oral sex. (For specific directions, see "Condoms," p. 110, or "Oral Dams," p. 116.)

How to get tested for it: If you suspect that you have gonorrhea (or want to get tested for it just in case), you can have your own doctor test you, go to your local health department, or go to a Planned Parenthood clinic. (For more information about testing sites, see *"Get tested regularly,"* p. 103.) You will be tested either by giving a urine sample or by having the doctor swab the area believed to be infected.

If you test positive: If you know for sure that you or your partner is infected, both of you should be treated. To avoid reinfecting yourselves, don't get it on again until you both have finished your antibiotics and the symptoms (if there were any) are gone.

Important side note: People who are infected with gonorrhea are often infected with chlamydia as well. If you or your partner test positive for gonorrhea, you both should be tested and/or treated for chlamydia.

Chlamydia

Signs a guy is experiencing symptoms of this STD: "Don't worry about the stuff dripping out of Mr. Happy. It's just pre-cum."

Signs you may have this STD: "Sure, it was unprotected sex, but I feel fine, so I'm sure there's nothing wrong."

Chlamydia statistic: In some parts of the country, one in ten adolescent females test positive for chlamydia. Most likely, you or someone you know has had (or does have) chlamydia. It is the most frequently reported bacterial STD in the United States.

Symptoms in men (should they occur): Only about half of men who are infected with chlamydia have symptoms, and they develop them within one to three weeks after being infected. Symptoms may include pain during urination, a creamy white liquid (that is not semen) dripping out of the penis, and sore or swollen testicles (déjà vu of gonorrhea).

Symptoms in women (should they occur): About 75 percent of women who have chlamydia don't have any symptoms. The few women who do develop them within one to three weeks of contracting this STD. The symptoms may include a slight burning during urination and a change in the smell or the texture of vaginal discharge.

Treatment: If you are infected with chlamydia, you can get treated with antibiotics, so, just like with gonorrhea, a diagnosed infection (especially caught early on) is not the end of the world.

Why it can really suck: Since most girls with chlamydia aren't in any physical discomfort, and those who are bothered by it can just get antibiotics, it may seem like chlamydia isn't that big of a deal. But the reason that chlamydia really sucks is that, if the infection is left untreated, about 40 percent of the time it will cause pelvic inflammatory disease, which can lead to permanent pain in your lower abdomen and vagina, infertility, and pregnancy complications. Also, if you are infected with chlamydia and then exposed to HIV, you are five times more likely to contract the virus.

How it is transmitted: Chlamydia is transmitted through unprotected sexual intercourse. Just like gonorrhea, you can get chlamydia when infected sexual fluids (mainly semen or vaginal discharge) come into contact with either a penis or vagina.

How to reduce your risk while still getting it on: To avoid getting chlamydia, use a condom every time you have sexual intercourse. (For more about condoms, see "Condoms," p. 110).

How to get tested for it: You can get tested for chlamydia at your doctor's office, a Planned Parenthood clinic, or your local health department. Just like with gonorrhea, there are both urine and swab tests for chlamydia; you either pee into a cup, or the doctor swabs your cervix (the opening to your uterus at the very end of your vaginal hole).

If you test positive: If you or a partner test positive for chlamydia, both of you should be treated with antibiotics. To avoid reinfecting yourselves, keep your hands off each other until you have finished your full course of antibiotics.

Crabs (Pubic Lice)

Signs a guy is experiencing symptoms of this STD: "These new boxers are really making my pubes itch. And dude, it looks like I have pubic dandruff!"

Signs you may have this STD: "Man, I've never had a bikini wax itch like this before!"

Crabs statistic: There are about three million cases of crabs in the United States every year.

Symptoms in men: Crabs are basically the perverted version of head lice. They're a very similar parasite, except that crabs prefer to be attached to pubic hair. When guys get crabs, most will notice their pubic region itching about five days after it becomes infested with the parasite.

Symptoms in women: When women get crabs, the symptoms are the same: an itchy pubic region. If you look closely, you can actually see the crabs or their eggs attached to the hair follicle. The crabs themselves are a whitish grey or rust color, and the eggs are a pearl-like color. Some people also notice little dark-bluish dots on their skin that are caused by the bites from the parasite.

Treatment: Crabs can be treated with a special shampoo that you can buy over the counter or have a doctor prescribe for you.

Why it can really suck: If you ever had lice as a kid, you may remember having to sit for hours while one of your parents raked through your hair with a fine-tooth comb, looking for nits. Imagine having to do that to your pubes. But as gross as crabs are, and as much of a pain as they are to treat, the good news is that they aren't actually harmful to your health—they just itch a lot.

How it is transmitted: You can catch crabs whenever some coarse hair on your body rubs against the coarse hair of someone who has crabs. Although this generally means pube-to-pube contact (even if you don't actually have sex), crabs can also live in eyebrows, eyelashes, armpit hair, or a guy's chest and facial hair. Since crabs can live independently off someone's body for twenty-four hours, you can also get it from towels, bed sheets, or clothing (usually bathing suits or underwear).

How to reduce your risk while still getting it on: Unfortunately, using a condom won't actually protect you from crabs (although you should always use one anyway). The only way to reduce your risk of getting crabs is to refrain from close contact with someone who may be infested (and don't borrow their dirty underwear).

How to get tested for it: Since crabs are visible to the naked eye, if your pubic region is itching and you can see the crabs or their eggs, you can diagnose yourself. If you're unsure whether or not you have crabs, have your doctor, someone at Planned Parenthood, or someone at a health clinic perform an examination.

If you test positive: If you do have crabs, you treat it the same way you would treat head lice. Wash your pubic hair with the treatment shampoo, and then pick out the little crab eggs. After you (and your partner) have been treated, wash everything that could be infested with crabs (basically anything you own that's not wood, metal, or plastic) in very hot water. If it can't be washed, then bag it up for two weeks. If after a week you still have symptoms, then both you and your partner should go through the same treatment drill again.

Not-so-important side note: I had head lice (not pubic) when I was nine, and for the next month my mom made everyone who entered the house wear a shower cap.

Herpes

Signs a guy is experiencing symptoms of this STD: "Forget the K-Y Jelly! I've got wet blisters on my shaft that are all the lubrication you need."

Signs you have this STD: "Baby doll, just don't mind the little pimply bumps around my pubic area."

Herpes statistics: It is estimated that as many as 20 percent of adults have genital herpes, but 90 percent don't know they have it because either they don't have symptoms or their symptoms are so minor they mistake it for something else. Most people are infected with herpes when they are teenagers.

Symptoms in men (should they occur): When a guy contracts the herpes virus, if he is going to develop symptoms (most people don't), it will probably happen within six to eight days (although it can take months or even a year). The first outbreak of symptoms is usually the most severe. Herpes can appear as one or more blisters that eventually open up and start oozing. They can also appear as cuts, pimples, bumps, or a rash on or around the penis. Some guys may mistake the symptoms of herpes as insect bites, ingrown hairs, or jock itch. For most guys who experience herpes outbreaks, the outbreak heals itself within two to twelve days.

Symptoms in women (should they occur): Girls who experience symptoms (and again, most don't) have symptoms similar to those of guys: blisters on or around the vagina that may feel like a paper cut. Girls may also experience what seems to be a rash, pimples, bumps, or cuts in this same region. Some girls may mistake their initial outbreak as a yeast infection, razor burn, or ingrown hairs. Also, girls may have pain and difficulty urinating.

Nongenital symptoms: Herpes sores or rashes can show up on the anus, butt, or thighs as well as the genitals, and some guys get them on their testicles. There are also herpes sores of the mouth (cold sores), a virus that many people contract when they are children. There is a chance that mouth herpes can be spread to the genitals, which is why making a guy use an oral dam when he goes down on you is so important. Although herpes is the most contagious when there is a visible sore, it's possible for the virus to be passed on whether or not a sore is present.

Treatment: If you are having a herpes outbreak, you can get ointment to help ease the pain of the sore. Also, a doctor can prescribe a medication that will reduce the severity and frequency of outbreaks.

Why it can really suck: Herpes sores can be painful, and while the individual sores do go away, you never get rid of the virus that causes them. Because you can't get rid of the virus, you can always pass it on to other people, and you can have outbreaks for the rest of your life.

How it is transmitted: The herpes virus is most contagious when the infected person is having an outbreak or right before an outbreak is about to occur. But even if the person with herpes is not having an outbreak, he or she can still pass on the virus. You can get herpes if your genitals or mouth come into contact with the infected area on someone else's body—generally, this means through unprotected oral sex or vaginal or anal intercourse.

How to reduce your risk while still getting it on: Using a condom all the time for intercourse (and a condom or oral dam during oral sex) will greatly reduce your risk of getting herpes. However, since herpes sores can break out in places not covered by a condom, even protected sex isn't 100 percent safe. If you're about to have sex with someone and he has any sort of visible rash or sore on his penis, *don't do it*, even with a condom. Although only a doctor can diagnose herpes for sure, it's best not to touch the area if it looks strange.

How to get tested for it: It is very difficult to determine whether someone has herpes. The majority of doctors and clinics can test someone for herpes only if he or she has a visible sore or rash. (Even then, the virus may not show up in the test.) If you develop a sore or rash that you think may be herpes, go to your doctor, a local Planned Parenthood, or the health department to have a physician swab the area. In order to get the most accurate results, you should try to see a doctor within forty-eight hours of the symptoms developing.

If you test positive: If you have an active herpes outbreak, there are medications that can make your symptoms less severe. However, the virus itself cannot be cured, which means that it stays in your body for your entire life. If you discover that you have herpes, you will need to tell any future sex partners that you have the virus, always use a condom, and abstain from sex if you have visible symptoms.

Even though about a fifth of the US population has herpes, finding out you have the virus can be both scary and depressing. Many people find it helpful to join a herpes support group (which you can join anonymously online) to talk about their concerns and fears. The following Web address has links to herpes chat rooms and support groups: http://www.ashastd.org/herpes/herpes_overview.cfm.

Genital Warts/Human Papillomavirus (HPV)

Signs a guy is experiencing symptoms of this STD: "My penis is bumped for your pleasure, baby! My hard grey-whitish lesions really get the girls going!"

Signs you may have this STD: "It's like a gray pearl necklace around my vagina—and look! There are even some soft pink ones, too!"

Genital warts/HPV statistic: Some experts estimate that as many as

75 percent of sexually active people in the United States will contract HPV in their lifetime.

Important clarification: HPV is the virus that causes genital warts; the warts themselves are a possible symptom of the virus. Some strains of genital HPV don't cause warts, and some can cause cervical cancer if undetected and untreated.

Important new development: You can now get a vaccine that will protect you against four strains of HPV (these four strains are responsible for causing about 70 percent of cervical cancer cases, and about 90 percent of genital warts cases). To find out more about getting vaccinated, ask your doctor, your local health department, or a Planned Parenthood clinic.

Symptoms in men (should they occur): If a guy is going to develop genital warts from being infected with HPV, he will usually do so within three weeks to three months of being infected. Some HPV-infected guys don't develop warts until years later, and most people never do. If the warts do develop, they are gray, whitish, or flesh-colored painless bumps that may be anywhere in the entire "boxer-short area."

Symptoms in women (should they occur): Girls who are infected with HPV may develop warts or have a Pap smear that comes back abnormal. (For more information about Pap smears, see "Infections and the Gyno," p. 31). As with guys, girls who develop warts do so within weeks or months (and in rare cases, years) after they are infected. Many HPV-infected girls never develop warts. If warts do appear, they will be gray or whitish painless bumps on the outside of the vagina or around the anus, or soft pink ones inside of the vagina.

Treatment: When someone develops genital warts as a result of being infected with HPV, a doctor can treat the warts themselves by burning or freezing them. Warts can also be treated with a prescription cream or be left to go away on their own. If you develop genital warts, *do not* try to treat the warts yourself by applying a general over-the-counter wart medication to your vagina. Not only will this "treatment" be ineffective (because warts on your fingers are very different from warts on your genitals), but also it could damage your vagina.

Why it can really suck: Although you can get rid of warts fairly easily, the virus that causes them takes years to go away, and there's no reliable test that determines when it actually has. There is a chance HPV can be detected in a girl through a Pap smear, but a Pap smear is not a definitive test. Many girls have HPV, and only some girls test positive for it; many guys have HPV, and they cannot be tested for it at all.

HPV is especially dangerous for girls because some of the strains of the virus cause cervical cancer. If you get regular Pap smears, your doctor can identify precancerous changes early on and actually prevent cervical cancer from developing.

How it is transmitted: HPV is spread mainly through unprotected sex. But because some guys may have warts on their testicles, anus, or groin (which are not covered by a condom), you can still catch HPV when using protection (although your risk is *much* lower). HPV is the most contagious when there are visible warts, but it can still be transmitted when there are no symptoms showing. You don't have to worry about getting genital warts from a guy who has a wart on his finger, since warts on fingers and warts on the genitals are caused by different strains of HPV.

How to reduce your risk while still getting it on: The best way to avoid catching HPV is to get vaccinated and—surprise, surprise—wear a condom when you're having sex. Use your common sense, and if you see a penis that has wartlike bumps on it, don't stick it inside of you.

How to get tested for it: As stated earlier, there is no test that accurately detects all people infected with HPV. (For guys, there's no test at all—although warts themselves can be visually diagnosed.) The strains of HPV that cause cervical cancer in women can be detected through Pap smears, which you can get at your regular doctor's office, a Planned Parenthood clinic, or a health center. Also, if you have any visible bumps, a doctor can examine them to determine whether they are genital warts caused by HPV. Unless a guy has visible signs of HPV that a doctor can examine (and remember, most don't), there is no way that a guy can be tested for the virus.

If you test positive: If a Pap smear comes back as abnormal, you will likely get further testing, more frequent Pap smears, and possibly laser treatment. As with any incurable STD, being diagnosed with HPV is something you must tell your current and future partners. In order to help prevent spreading the virus, you should always use a condom. And if you smoke, quitting will help your immune system fight HPV.

HIV/AIDS

Important clarification: Human immunodeficiency virus (HIV) is a virus that affects a person's immune system by attacking his or her T cells (which fight off disease). People are said to have acquired immunodeficiency syndrome (AIDS) when their T cell count falls below 200 (most healthy people have between 500 and 1,600 T cells), or they get a serious HIV-related illnesses. Although many people with AIDS get very sick, people with HIV can look completely healthy on the outside. Some people who have HIV can go many years without any sign that they're infected.

HIV/AIDS statistic: In the United States, it used to be that homosexual men were the main group of people infected with HIV. But now it is estimated that half of all new HIV infections occur in people thirteen to twenty-four years old, and half of those infections occur in women.

Symptoms in men: Within days or weeks of exposure to HIV, men may develop flu-like symptoms including fever, fatigue, a rash, headaches, swollen lymph nodes, or a sore throat. Some men have no symptoms early on. After the initial infection, there may be a long period with no symptoms at all (in some cases, ten years or longer). Eventually, if a guy does not receive treatment, he can develop the following symptoms: rapid weight loss, dry cough, night sweats, fatigue, swollen lymph glands, diarrhea, white spots in the mouth, and pneumonia. As HIV progresses even further, especially without treatment, more life-threatening diseases develop.

Symptoms in women: HIV symptoms in women are the same as those described for men. In addition, HIV-infected women may also get frequent and severe vaginal infections, pelvic inflammatory disease, or abnormal Pap smears.

Treatment: There are now drugs available that allow people infected with HIV/AIDS to live longer and healthier lives. But these drugs are expensive, they can have many side effects, and they cannot cure you. Most people infected with HIV eventually die from AIDS-related causes, although life expectancy is increasing due to new medications.

How it is transmitted: You can get HIV/AIDS by having unprotected intercourse, anal intercourse, or oral sex with someone who is infected (although your risk of contracting HIV from oral sex is fairly low). You cannot get it from kissing, hugging, or sharing food with someone who is infected with HIV.

How to reduce your risk of contracting it: The only way to avoid HIV completely is by not having sex. If you are having sex, be sure that your partner has tested negative for HIV (and that, when he got tested, he followed the correct testing procedures discussed below). No matter what, always use a condom when having anal sex or sexual intercourse (and to be even safer, use a condom or an oral dam during oral sex). Using a condom doesn't mean putting one on right before a guy cums; it means that, before there is any kind of contact with his penis in your mouth, vagina, or anus, it has been covered with a condom.

How to get tested for it: In order for an HIV test to be accurate, you must get tested eight weeks after the last time you have had unprotected sex. (It can take this long for the antibodies to show up in your blood.) When you get tested, you can have a blood test, a urine test, or a saliva test. Some tests give you results in twenty minutes, and others take one to two weeks. You can get tested for HIV at your doctor's office, your health center, or Planned Parenthood. (For more information, see *"Get tested regularly,"* p. 103.)

What to do if you test positive: If you have tested positive for HIV, you probably want to talk with someone about it. If you don't want to talk to a family member or a friend, you can speak with a counselor at the National AIDS Hotline at 1-800-232-4636. You should also inform all of your previous partners that you are HIV positive, and visit a doctor who can advise you on living with the virus.

Other (Not Very Common) STDs

Both hepatitis B and syphilis are STDs that should be fairly low on your list of concerns. Although both are very serious diseases that can be fatal, syphilis is pretty uncommon, and hepatitis B is preventable through a vaccine.

What to know about hepatitis B: If you have a doctor that you see regularly, then chances are that you have already been vaccinated against hepatitis B. Ideally, you should get the vaccination before you start having any kind of sex, since hepatitis B can be transmitted through vaginal sex, anal sex, and, very rarely, oral sex. If you haven't already been vaccinated, then you should do so as soon as possible; once you are infected with hepatitis

B, you are infected for life, and the virus can be life-threatening. The vaccinations are a series of three shots that are pretty painless. If, for any reason, you feel uncomfortable about asking your regular doctor for the vaccine, you can get vaccinated at most local health centers.

What you should know about syphilis: Syphilis is a fairly uncommon STD that can be treated if it's caught early but can be fatal if it's not. Although it is uncommon in the United States as a whole, it is more common in the South, in African American populations, and in men who have sex with other men. You can get syphilis by having unprotected oral, anal, or vaginal sex with someone who is infected.

Syphilis comes in three phases. During the first phase, there will be a painless sore, which will disappear on its own. This sore will usually appear between ten and ninety days from when you were exposed to the disease and will go away in one to five weeks. During the second phase (which can occur as late as six months after the first), a skin rash develops, along with flu-like symptoms. The rash may be reddish brown and appear on the palms of your hands, soles of your feet, neck, head, and torso. Infections that progress to the third stage affect the heart, brain, and eyes, and can be deadly. If you think you may have been exposed to syphilis, or if you notice any of the preceding symptoms, let your doctor know. Your doctor can give you a blood test to see whether you have syphilis, and then can treat you with antibiotics. If syphilis is detected in the first or second stage, you can be cured of the disease, and your body will not be permanently damaged. If syphilis is detected in the third stage, although you can still be cured, any damage that has already been done to your organs cannot be reversed.

WHY "I'VE BEEN TESTED" CAN MEAN "I'M FULL OF SHIT"

If you have not yet heard the phrases "We don't need to use a condom, baby—I've been tested" or "What are you worried about?—I'm clean," you will. In fact, I'll venture to guess that you'll hear them a lot. But what does being tested or being "clean" really mean anyway? There are many STDs out there; when a guy says he has "been tested," is he saying that he's been tested for *all* of them?

On a guy, genital warts (HPV) can be diagnosed only visually, so in order for him to have been tested, he must have first had symptoms. Herpes is almost always diagnosed visually as well, which again means that a guy who has been tested for it probably had a physical sign of the virus. If a guy has really "been tested" for genital warts or herpes, it means that, at some point, he had unexplained bumps, sores, or a rash somewhere around his genitals.

For your partner to have been truly tested for *everything* possible, he must have gone eight weeks without any sexual contact; have gotten tested for syphilis, hepatitis B, chlamydia, gonorrhea, and HIV; and have no unidentified bumps anywhere on his penis, anus, or testicles (one hell of a thorough examination). And even then, there's still a chance he is carrying the HPV or herpes virus (which also happen to be the most common STDs). Basically, being "tested" doesn't mean he's STD free; it just means that he doesn't have any of the STDs you can easily test for. And being "clean" is almost always an assumption rather than a fact.

The scariest thing about STDs is that the majority of people who spread them don't know they have them. Because 50 to 75 percent of people who have an STD don't have any symptoms, you can't tell that someone is free of diseases just by looking at him or her, his Johnson, or her vagina.

LONG STORY SHORT

In a nutshell, there are many STDs out there, and many people have them. Because vaginas have more fragile skin than penises, it's twice as easy for you to get an STD from a guy than vice versa. The only truly safe sex act is masturbation (or abstinence, but that's not sex at all). So when you have sex, you have to be very careful.

If you're sexually active, there is no absolute guarantee that you will be able to avoid STDs completely. However, you can *greatly* reduce your risk of contracting them or having them cause permanent damage to your body. To best protect yourself, consistently take the following precautions.

Have your partner wear a condom (and use a condom or oral dam for oral sex). Since STDs can affect the entire pubic region (everything from the anus to the upper thigh), it would really be safest if we all had sex in wet suits—or at least biker shorts. But because that would be a little strange, we have to settle for a condom. Using a condom doesn't mean letting a possibly infected penis rub itself all over you, and then covering it right before it slips in. To most effectively protect yourself from STDs, you have to put a condom on a penis before it touches your body.

Using a condom is the number-one most important thing you can do to maintain your sexual health. And just like exercising every day and avoiding fried food, simply knowing something is healthy doesn't always make it an easy thing to do. As difficult as it may be to make *every* partner use a condom *every* time, I promise you will never look back on an experience and think, "Man, if only I had not used a condom that time, everything would have worked out so much better." With as many gray areas as there are with sex, whether or not it's a good idea to use a condom is always black and white. (For more information about condoms, see p. 110.)

Get tested regularly. Deciding to get tested for an STD can be scary because it means admitting there's a chance (no matter how remote) that you may have one. For the longest time, I refused to get an HIV test because I didn't want to spend four days freaking out that it was going to come back positive. It was less emotionally taxing to just assume that I was fine.

As stressful as being tested for an STD may be, knowing early on that you have one can prevent permanent damage to your reproductive system as well as prevent you from passing it along to someone else. Getting tested for STDs is something that you can do fairly easily (and your parents don't have to know if you would rather they didn't). If you are comfortable with the possibility of your parents knowing that you are getting tested for STDs, then tell your regular doctor about your sexual history, and he or she will decide which tests are appropriate to run. (Many doctors can't or won't tell a girl's parents that she is being tested for STDs, but, depending on the state you live in, and the doctor, your parents *could* find out.)

If you believe that your parents absolutely cannot know that you are getting tested for STDs, then you can receive confidential STD tests at most Planned Parenthoods or public health departments. To find a Planned Parenthood close to you, or to make an appointment, contact the organization at 1-800-230-7526. You will be scheduled for an office visit where you will meet with a doctor to discuss which STD tests should be run. This will cost you about $30 to $160, depending on which tests are performed.

You can also get privately tested for STDs at your local health department (although it may not have as many testing options). Getting tested at your health department will be very inexpensive, and they may even run some tests for free. To find out where your closest department of health is located, call 1-800-232-4636, or look it up yourself at http://www.hivtest.org.

If you have had unprotected sex, then you should look into testing options. If you are unsure whether or not you're at risk, any place that does testing will have counselors who can answer your questions. Sure, being tested for STDs is no one's idea of an awesome after-school activity, but if you catch a curable STD early on, you can prevent permanent damage to your reproductive system and overall health. If your condom-use record is less than perfect, you can't go back in time and change the fact that you didn't use one. Your only option for protection after unprotected sex is getting tested and using a condom in the future.

Keep an eye on your vagina and a mental note on your sex partners. It's true that many people who have an STD don't show any symptoms, but some people do show symptoms, and most of the time those symptoms are very subtle. The better you keep tabs on what your vagina looks, smells, and feels like, the better you'll recognize when something is a little off. If something is even slightly funky with your vagina, don't wait it out to see if the problem goes away; the symptom itself might. The actual STD (if it is one) won't go away unless you have it treated (assuming that it's curable). If you notice any weird bumps, odors, burning, or itching (even if it is very subtle), go see a doctor. It may turn out to be nothing, but when it comes to your vaginal health, you always want to be sure.

Since many people with STDs don't have symptoms, as closely as you monitor your vagina, you also have to monitor your risk. If you're recounting your sexual experiences and realize you had unprotected sex with Mr. "I've Been In Everyone's Pants," you should get screened for STDs even if your vagina seems fine. And really, even if you had unprotected sex with a guy who's done it with "only a couple of girls," you're still at risk for having an STD. (Think about it: he's had sex with three girls, who have each had sex with three guys, who have each had sex with three girls—and pretty soon that number is getting up there.) If you have had any unprotected sex, it's a good idea to make an appointment with a doctor to discuss STD testing. The earlier you treat an STD, the less damage it will cause to your health, and the fewer people you will infect.

Ask about your partner's sexual history. The "how many people have you been with" talk isn't easy, especially since the answer to that question is more complicated than a number. A guy's "number" only refers to how many people he's had sex with, not how likely it is that he's carrying an STD. Say one guy has had sex with ten girls, but he used a condom every time, and another guy has had sex with two, but he didn't use a condom, and one of the girls had been around the block more times than the postman. In this case, the guy who at first may have seemed more selective because he had sex with only two girls is actually the one who is more likely to have an STD.

In order to get the full picture of a guy's sexual past, you need to know how many people he's had sex with, how "experienced" the girls he slept with were, and whether or not he used a condom. If you don't feel comfortable asking him these questions, you may want to reconsider your decision to have sex with him.

You don't have to talk about your sexual history on the first date, but don't wait until you're about to have sex with someone to bring it up. Chances are, if you wait that long, you won't bring it up at all. Maybe you think that knowing a guy's sexual past won't change your decision to sleep with him, but you never know for sure. Some fairly young guys are *very* experienced—if a prospective partner told you he had been with thirty-some girls, would you still definitely want to sleep with him? Even if a guy's experience isn't going to influence your decision to have sex with him, you should at least know the risk you are taking by doing it.

Never assume that it's OK to have unprotected sex with a guy who has a seemingly innocent sexual history. Guys may not tell you (or even know) how many times they or their previous partners engaged in unprotected sex. Memories can be both faulty and selective, and there are always guys who will flat out lie. No matter how informed you are about whom your partner has been with, you should always protect yourself by using a condom.

WORST-CASE SCENARIO

Although you may do everything you can to protect yourself from getting an STD, there is always a possibility that you could get one anyway. Luckily, many STDs are curable after they are detected, and the severity of the incurable ones can be lessened through treatment. Clearly, most people don't advertise that they have an STD—especially if it's one that can't be cured—but thousands of people contract one every day. If you find out that you have an STD, *you are not alone*. No one *wants* an STD, but if you do get one (and it can't be cured), you learn to live with it. Below is the story of a young woman dealing with herpes.

LIVING WITH HERPES: BY J.A.G.

I am a twenty-four-year-old woman with herpes. "Ewww," you might say—and I might even agree with you. But as gross as it may be, it's not the end of my life; it's just another one of those hurdles that has been placed before me. Is it easy? No, I would never say it is easy—although I know that the extent to which it will affect my life is determined solely by how much I let it dominate my thoughts.

When I was first diagnosed, I felt like the world was tumbling down. I was convinced that I would never have a boyfriend again. It wasn't long before those feelings subsided, and I met an amazing guy who didn't think twice about it. He knew he liked me and felt that my condition was not a reason to stay away from me. My honesty was something he admired, and he was willing to commit to me if I was willing to stay honest. Although I know that not every guy will respond so positively, I also know that there are people out there who won't judge me based on a common permanent condition.

The best advice I can give to anyone who has been recently diagnosed is *stay positive and love yourself*. Herpes will slow you down, but not in a bad way. You learn to proceed with caution. There is no easy way to disclose your condition, but you must do it whenever you are getting intimate with someone. Sometimes you may face rejection, and that will be difficult. But the less you define yourself by an STD, the more likely it is that other people will be able to look beyond it when getting to know you. Life is short; don't waste it feeling sorry for yourself.

FURTHER INFORMATION ABOUT STDS AND STD PREVENTION

* American Social Health Association (general information about STDs): http://www.ashastd.org

* American Social Health Association (information for teens about STDs): http://www.iwannaknow.org

* The Body (a complete HIV/AIDS resource): http://www.the body.com

* Centers for Disease Control and Prevention (information from the CDC about STDs): http://www.cdc.gov/std

* Centers for Disease Control and Prevention's twenty-four-hour STD Hotline: 1-800-232-4636

* Coalition for Positive Sexuality (information about safer sex): http://www.positive.org/JustSayYes/safesex.html

* Information about anonymous HIV-testing sites near you: 1-888-PEACE-4U

* Sex, Etc. (information about STDs): http://www.sexetc.org/index.php

Chapter 8

Contraception and Protection

Rubber Dicky, You're the One

When I started using birth control, it felt like my rite of passage to being a woman. It wasn't the act of having sex that made me feel older; it was the burden of having to protect myself from getting pregnant or getting an STD.

When my friends and I talked about sex, we often talked more about the brand of contraceptive pill and condom we used rather than the actual act. We carried around our hard pink cases of pills and our three-packs of Trojans with the same pride as we jingled our car keys the first day we got our licenses. There was something empowering about having regular, responsible sex.

But soon enough, using protection was no longer exciting. It hit like the realization you have the second week back in school after summer vacation—wait a minute, this kinda sucks. The sense of pride that we once took in using protection turned into complaints:

"I don't like the way I feel on birth control pills."

"John doesn't like condoms."

"Ewww—a diaphragm, are you kidding me?"

As the novelty of using birth control and having protected sex vanished, so did many of our safer sex habits. As a result, a few of my friends got genital warts, and many of them had close brushes with pregnancy.

It would be a lie to say that there's a perfect form of birth control that will protect you from pregnancy and STDs without any drawbacks. But whatever downsides there are to using contraception, it's much better than getting pregnant or contracting an STD. Most doctors recommend using birth control pills and also a condom: the condom for protection from STDs and birth control pills for added protection from pregnancy. This chapter is about different forms of contraception and what to do about their downsides.

CONDOMS

I remember watching my seventh grade teacher put a condom on a banana, and it seemed so simple. She didn't have to ask the banana if it minded wearing a condom. She didn't have to counter complaints about condoms ruining the intimacy of being in a fruit bowl. And if the condom happened to rip a little, so what? It was just an unprotected fruit. At the time, my female classmates and I had no idea that putting a condom on a penis wasn't going to be as easy.

You may have heard that condoms reduce guys' physical sensation during sex. This can be true. Luckily, many guys understand that while condoms may make sex slightly less pleasurable, using one is still better than the risk of getting a girl pregnant or contracting an STD. One guy told me recently, "If a girl doesn't ask to use a condom, I wear one anyway. And if she tells me not to, then I wear two because who knows how many guys she has had unprotected sex with?" Wearing two condoms at once is actually a bad idea because it can cause them to break more easily, but the guy made a good point: not only are many guys willing to use condoms, but some also get alarmed by a girl who doesn't want to use one. After all, using a condom doesn't just protect you, it protects him as well.

As widespread as condom use may be, it's possible you may find yourself in a situation where you're about to have sex, and the issue of using a condom has not been mentioned. If this happens, don't be afraid to ask a guy to use one. A guy isn't going to like you more or think you're a "laid-back chick" because you don't ask him to use a condom.

Many guys will respect you more for setting ground rules for your sexual encounter and for taking the responsibly to keep both of you safe.

If you find that asking a guy to use a condom throws him into a hissy fit about "ruining his sexual experience," keep the following things in mind.

If he only cares about "his sexual experience," then the sex is going to suck for you. If a guy knows that you're uncomfortable having sex without a condom yet pressures you to do it anyway, then he's only interested in his own sexual gratification and may as well be screwing a cantaloupe. A guy needs to respect your feelings and, most important, do *whatever* it will take to make you feel comfortable during a sexual encounter. If he doesn't care about making you feel comfortable enough to enjoy sex, he doesn't care about you, and you probably shouldn't be sleeping with him.

He's getting laid/getting a blow job. Any guy who is having sex (or receiving oral sex) should not complain about any reduced sensation

"This guy may as well be having sex with himself"

caused by a condom. (Well, he can complain about it, as long as he wears one anyway.) Every day, millions of men engage in sex acts while using a condom, but they still enjoy the experience, and they still get off. Condoms may reduce what guys feel a little bit, but younger guys can probably stand to feel less and last a little longer anyway (at least as far as intercourse is concerned). If a guy really hates condoms so much, he's always free to go home and jack off—not wearing one.

It may be more likely that he has an STD. Along the same line of thinking as the "I wear two" guy quoted earlier: any guy who objects to using a condom with you has probably objected to using a condom with someone else. Basically, he may not be the freshest fish in the pond. The more unprotected sex he has had, the more likely it is that he has an STD, and the more important it is that you make him use a condom.

So You Don't Like Rubbers

Some girls are hesitant to use condoms because *they* don't like using them (not because *their partner* doesn't like using them). I know a few of my friends complain that they don't like the feeling of rubber inside of them, or that putting on a condom is awkward and disruptive to the sexual encounter. The following is a list of common concerns about condoms and what you can do about them.

Using a condom isn't as intimate because there isn't skin-to-skin contact. Sure, when you use a condom, the skin of your vagina is not touching the skin of a guy's penis. But assuming that you're having sex naked, there are many other bare parts for you and your partner to enjoy. The passion and intimacy of sex has much more to do with how you and your partner are kissing and touching each other than whether or not there is a piece of latex covering a his penis. If the sex you're having isn't passionate or fulfilling enough for you, blaming the condom is barking up the wrong tree.

Using a condom irritates your vagina. Some girls find that certain types of condoms make their vagina sting. If you have this problem, it's most likely the lubrication on the condom, and not the condom itself, that is giving you trouble. Most condom companies make unlubricated, lubricated, and spermicidal lubricated condoms. Your best bet is to use con-

doms that are lubricated *without* spermicide or ones that are not lubricated at all. (If unlubricated condoms are too dry for you, use K-Y Jelly
for lubrication.)

Putting on a condom is disruptive to the sexual encounter. Probably the
most common complaint about using condoms is that it disrupts sex.
The thing is, the whole process of putting on a condom takes about three
seconds. And if you're the one putting the condom on your partner, two
of those seconds are spent touching his penis. Putting on a condom takes
about the same amount of time as taking off your shirt and probably
much less time than taking off your bra. But you probably wouldn't be
tempted to go braless so that your bra wouldn't disrupt your hookups.

The difference is that most people consider taking off clothing as
foreplay but, for whatever reason, don't look at putting on a condom in
the same way. You should look at using a condom as a part of sex, not a
disruption of it. If you're putting the condom on your partner, think of
it as a two-second hand job. And if he is putting it on himself, continue
to touch and kiss him, and that way you're not stopping any action. If
you're concerned about disruptions, just make sure that there is a
condom near the bed. The actual act of putting a condom on doesn't have
to feel disruptive at all.

Putting on a condom is really awkward. Putting on a condom should
be a fairly quick and painless experience. If it feels awkward, it's probably because you're taking too long to put it on. When the time comes
to put on the condom, don't play "condom hot potato" and pass it back
and forth. If you want to be the one to put it on, open the condom and
do it. If you feel uncomfortable with putting a condom on a guy, then
hand it to him and have him do it.

It may be a good idea to practice putting on a condom by rolling
one down a banana (like we did in my seventh grade class). The more
confident you are in your ability to put on a condom quickly and correctly, the less awkward you will feel when it comes time to use one. No
matter how uneasy you may feel about condoms, putting one on can't be
more uncomfortable than having to tell your next partner that you have
an STD or informing your current partner that you're pregnant.

How to *Correctly* Use a Condom

You would think that the only way to mess up using a condom is to not use one. But condoms actually malfunction regularly because people aren't following correct condom procedure. I realize that the idea of "correct condom usage" may seem unnecessarily anal, but there are many ways to screw up with condoms. Paying attention to using a condom the right way is almost as important as deciding to use one in the first place. After all, if a condom slips off or breaks, you are still at risk for contracting an STD and getting pregnant. To increase the effectiveness of condoms, follow these instructions.

1. Store condoms at room temperature. Exposing condoms to extreme temperatures makes them more likely to break. This means no glove compartments and no wallets. If all you have is a smushed-up wallet condom, you're best off waiting to have sex. But if you're going to have sex anyway, a beat-up condom is still better than no condom at all.

2. Check the date. Since we don't eat condoms, it's not intuitive to check the date on the wrapper before using one. But condoms can "go bad" if they aren't used before the "use by" date. Be sure that your condoms have not expired—especially if you bought them out of a machine in a bathroom or at a run-down gas station. If you have to rub the dust off a condom just to be able to read the brand name, you should definitely check the date before getting busy.

3. Tame the Tarzan act. When you're really turned on, some actions that might otherwise seem creepy and dumb seem like really good ideas. To add some sexiness to the action of putting on a condom, it may be tempting to rip the condom open with your teeth, let out a growl, then pounce on top of your partner like a cavewoman. Unfortunately, biting or violently ripping open the condom package might tear the condom as well as the packaging. You can still growl and leap if you really want to, but be delicate with the condom.

4. Stay out of the kitchen when looking for a lubricant. If you have ever gotten a body part stuck in between poles on a banister, you know that lubricating your stuck body part with butter helps it slide out a little easier. When you are having sex, you may want to use a lubricant to help the penis slide *in* a little better and to avoid chafing. Using lubrication also decreases the chances that the condom will break. (Just make sure to put it on the *outside* of the condom.) K-Y Jelly or any lubrication that says "water-based" on the package is fine to use with a condom; just stay away from food shortening, petroleum jelly, or anything with an oil base. Oil weakens the latex of a condom and increases the chances that it will break. So when looking for lubrication, leave the butter in the fridge.

5. Put on the condom before *any* penetration. Don't start having sex and then stop to put on a condom right before the guy has an orgasm. First of all, that's not protecting yourself from STDs or completely protecting yourself from pregnancy. Second of all, if you're worried about the disruption of putting on a condom *before* you start having sex, you definitely don't want to put one on *while* you're having sex.

6. Leave room for the little soldiers. When putting on a condom, pinch the tip to make sure there are no air pockets, and roll it from the top all the way down to the base of the penis. (The extra room at the tip is so a guy's semen doesn't bust right through.) If the condom isn't rolling down easily, try flipping it over because you may be trying to use it inside out. Although this sounds like a total airhead thing to do, it happens more often than you may think, since many sexual encounters take place in the dark.

7. When he runs out of fuel, stop driving! Sometimes when a guy has an orgasm sooner than he would like, he'll continue to have sex after he ejaculates to avoid the label of a "two-pump chump." This is a problem because the in-and-out motion of sex pushes the sperm toward the base of the condom and makes it more

likely that some will leak out. After a guy has finished, he needs to pull out. (If you want to continue having sex—and the guy is capable of still going—take the first condom off and put on another one.)

8. Grip the base of the penis when pulling out. After ejaculating, the penis acts very much like the witch in *The Wizard of Oz*: "I'm melting! I'm melting!" And as the penis gets softer and smaller, the condom gets looser. So if you don't hold the condom at the base when withdrawing, you run the risk of the condom slipping off.

9. Get rid of the condom. Condoms are made to be used only once. Even if your partner didn't ejaculate into the condom, once a condom has been unrolled, it needs to be thrown out. You can't roll the condom back up and try to put it on again later. If you do that, it's likely that the condom will tear. Besides, if you find it awkward to put a rolled-up condom onto a penis, try attempting to pull on a condom that has already been unrolled.

ORAL DAMS

An "oral dam" sounds like a metal contraption you'd get along with headgear when you have braces. But as unsexy as the name may be, an actual oral dam is nothing as bulky and awkward as the names suggests. Oral dams are sheets of latex that you hold over your vagina to protect yourself from STDs when someone is giving you oral sex (or when you're going down on a girl).

Receiving oral sex puts you at risk for contracting gonorrhea, hepatitis B (if you're not vaccinated), syphilis, herpes, and possibly HIV (although the chance of contracting HIV from someone going down on you is slim). The STD you should really worry about contracting from unprotected oral sex is genital herpes (since it is incurable, and herpes is fairly common). Using an oral dam greatly reduces your risk of getting an STD from someone going down on you. To use an oral dam, follow these easy steps.

1. Get an oral dam. You can buy oral dams at most drugstores, health departments, or Planned Parenthood clinics. Because you may not be able to predict when you are going to be having oral sex, it's best to pick some up to have around just in case.

2. Find/make an oral dam. Although it's always best to use an actual oral dam, if you don't have one around and you're going to have oral sex, you can use plastic wrap (which actually works very well) or cut the tip off a condom and then slit it up the side.

3. Rinse it and check it. Before you use the oral dam, you may want to rinse it off (so that your partner doesn't have to be licking the baby powder that coats the dam). Give the dam a good look-over to make sure there are no holes. If you know that you are going to be having oral sex, you can always rinse it off beforehand and set it aside for later. You don't *have* to rinse off the dam, so if it is in the heat of the moment and you don't want to (or can't) run to a sink, it's not a big deal. Your partner may get a little bit of powder in his mouth, but the dam will still work fine.

4. Hold the dam in place. To use the dam, hold the latex over your entire vaginal area and let your partner do his thing. Or, if you want to have your hands free, your partner can hold the dam in place for you. If you're worried about oral sex not being as pleasurable with an oral dam, add some lubrication between the latex and your vagina, and it will feel more like a bare tongue.

5. Pick a side and stick to it. The most common way that people mess up when using an oral dam is by flipping it over. The whole idea of the dam is to keep your vaginal fluids on one side and his saliva on the other, so switching sides halfway through defeats the whole purpose of using it in the first place.

6. Throw it away. Once you are done with the dam, you have to throw it out. Although oral dams kind of look like something that you could rinse off and reuse, they are made to be used only once.

Using an oral dam may feel a little awkward at first, but after a few times it will become a normal part of your sexual routine—just like using a condom.

Birth Control Pills (Oral Contraceptives)

I was pretty hesitant to take birth control pills when I first started having sex. I had heard horror stories that they made some girls crazy, made others nauseous, and made all girls gain weight. So when my doctor offered to prescribe them for me, I told her, "Thanks, but no thanks." I told her what I was afraid might happen, and to my surprise, she assured me that the side effects I was worried about were false, rare, or avoidable.

Taking birth control pills won't protect you from STDs, but if you take them consistently, they're an extremely effective way to protect yourself from getting pregnant. But because so many girls are misinformed about the side effects and hassles of birth control pills, some refuse to take them. The following are five reasons for why you may be hesitant to take birth control pills, and why these concerns aren't much to worry about at all.

I don't want my parents to know I'm having sex. In a perfect world, girls would tell their mothers, "I'm going to have sex," and their mothers would respond with, "Wonderful, dear. We'll get you on birth control, find some scented candles, and buy you a bag of rose petals." In reality, many girls feel that their mother's response would be more along the lines of "You're grounded."

Even if you can't tell your parents that you're having sex, it doesn't mean that you can't get birth control pills. In many states, your doctor is not allowed to tell your parents that she has prescribed birth control pills for you (although the pills may show up on a bill that your parents pay). You can ask your doctor if she can, and will, prescribe birth control pills for you without telling your parents. If you don't trust your regular doctor, or just don't want to talk to her about sex, you can get birth control pills from a Planned Parenthood clinic. (For more information, call 1-800-230-PLAN.)

I don't want to get fat. Many girls are hesitant to go on birth control pills because of the "weight gain" side effect. But, according to the American College of Obstetricians and Gynecologists, as many women lose weight on the pill as gain weight. Of all the girls I know who are on the pill, *none* of them attribute any change of weight to the fact that they are on birth control. Many have said that the pill has made their boobs bigger though—but they weren't too unhappy about that one.

Many girls naturally gain weight as they get older. If a girl doesn't start taking birth control pills until she is in her late teens, she may gain weight and assume that it's because of the pill. In actuality, her weight gain is a result of her age, her metabolism slowing down, and the fact that she is no longer growing. Girls in their teens and twenties gain weight, and that goes for girls who take the pill as well as those who don't.

I don't want to feel like crap or go crazy. The birth control pills on the market now are only a fraction as strong as the ones that were available some twenty to thirty years ago—but much of the pill's bad reputation today comes from how strong it *used* to be. According to the American College of Obstetricians and Gynecologists, the possible side effects of taking birth control pills *can* include headaches, mood changes, breast tenderness, irregular bleeding, and missed periods. But many girls are able to take them without these problems. When a girl does experience side effects, they will likely go away after her body gets more used to the birth control pills (usually three months).

If you start taking birth control and you're having side effects that aren't going away (or you don't want to wait for them to), you can always switch to a different brand or stop using hormonal contraception all together. There are many kinds of birth control pills available that have different hormone levels and combinations; you're bound to find *one* that agrees with you. If you discuss your problems on one type of pill with your doctor, she is likely to find another pill that will work better for you.

I don't want long-term health complications. Some girls have been told that birth control pills are bad for their health, that they cause cancer or infertility, and that they are generally risky. The American College of Obstetricians and Gynecologists, however, says birth control pills do not cause cancer, they don't make women infertile, and they're risky only for women over thirty-five who smoke.

There are many studies that have examined the link between birth control pills and cancer. The majority of them found that the pill does not increase the chance a girl will develop cervical or breast cancer. Many studies have also found that birth control pills may even make girls *less* likely to get endometrial cancer.

Some women who have taken birth control pills may have infertility problems, but their problems were not *caused* by taking the pill. You may have heard a story about a woman who took birth control pills for fifteen years and then couldn't get pregnant. While the story may be true, it doesn't mean that taking birth control pills was *the reason* that the woman couldn't get pregnant. There may also be a woman who was a vegetarian for fifteen years and then couldn't get pregnant, but it doesn't mean that being vegetarian caused her infertility. Many women have difficulty getting pregnant; whether or not they have taken the pill is irrelevant.

I can barely remember to get dressed every day; there's no chance I'm going to remember to take a pill. Remembering to take your birth control pill is not as difficult as you may think. If you pair it with something you do each day—like brushing your teeth—it becomes part of your routine. Some girls I know set the alarm on their cell phone or watch to remind them to take their pill.

If you're really worried about remembering to take a pill every day, you can get "the ring," which you insert into your vagina and change only once a month. No matter how absentminded you may be, there will be a way to make hormonal contraception work for you. To find out more about your contraceptive options, speak with your doctor or call Planned Parenthood at 1-800-230-PLAN.

(Note: Some medications can interfere with the effectiveness of birth control pills. So if you decide to get on birth control pills, be sure to tell your doctor you are taking them before she prescribes you any other medication.)

Other Types of Contraception

✳ Depo-Provera: Depo-Provera is a shot that your doctor gives you every three months with hormones similar to those in birth control pills. It very effectively prevents pregnancy because, as long as you get it every three months, there's no way to screw it up. The major problem with this method is that, if you're experiencing uncomfortable side effects, you have to wait three months for them to go away, as opposed to the pill, which you can just stop taking. The side effects you may experience include bleeding between periods, depression, and weight gain. Another problem with the Depo shot is that it can reduce bone density (which eventually causes osteoporosis, a common problem for many women). Because of this, most doctors don't recommend that young women use it for an extended period. And like birth control pills, the Depo shot doesn't protect you from STDs.

✳ Diaphragm: A diaphragm is a little flexible cup that holds spermicide and is inserted into your vagina. You must put the diaphragm into your vagina no more than two hours before you're going to have sex. After you have sex, you must let it sit for eight hours, and then remove it and wash it out. If you're at all squeamish about sexual fluids or sticking your fingers far up into your vagina, then a diaphragm is not for you. Also, it won't protect you from getting STDs.

✳ Female condom: A female condom is more expensive than a male condom, harder to find, harder to use, and less reliable. But if you're not willing to ask the guy you're sleeping with to use a condom, or are unable to convince him, a female condom is your next-best option for STD protection. Although it's always a smart idea to use two types of contraception, never use a female condom at the same time as a male condom; they will get entangled with one another, make a mess, and be completely ineffective. If you are going to use a female condom, be sure to thoroughly read the instructions that come with it before you plan on using it.

PULLING OUT: NOT CONTRACEPTION (OR PROTECTION FROM STDS)

Pulling out—when a couple has unprotected sex and then the guy "pulls out" right before he ejaculates—is about as reliable as your horoscope. Sure, you can use it anytime, anywhere, and with absolutely no preparation, but it's very easy to get pregnant when using pulling out as contraception. Besides, a birth control method commonly referred to as "pull and pray" should raise a red flag. If you have to "pray" that you're not pregnant, that's a good sign that your contraceptive method isn't very reliable.

Pulling out isn't a dependable contraceptive option because, before a guy has an orgasm and ejaculates, small amounts of precum drip out of his penis. Maybe you've heard the saying, "Sex is like basketball: you dribble before you shoot," meaning that, even if he was able to pull out before he had an orgasm, you could still get pregnant from his precum. And if his orgasm takes him by surprise, and he waits just a second too long to pull out, about 600 million sperm have been launched up your vagina. To get pregnant, only one has to reach its destination. How's that for odds?

Although pulling out is not reliable protection from pregnancy, and not any protection from STDs, if one day you find yourself having unprotected sex, pulling out is better than nothing. I look at it this way: it's a bad idea to jump off a building, but if you've already jumped, you may as well open your parachute.

THE RHYTHM METHOD: ALSO NOT CONTRACEPTION

You may have heard that if you have sex right before or during your period, you don't have to worry about getting pregnant. This myth comes from "the rhythm method," a form of "birth control" in which girls predict when they will be ovulating (the days when they can get pregnant), and they don't have sex around that time. Then, for the rest of the month, they have sex without any kind of protection.

While it is true that there are only a few days each month that a girl can get pregnant, it's also true that the time a girl is the most fertile occurs about twelve days before her *next* period. The problem then is that no girl's period is completely predictable. So unless you know the exact day you're going to get your next period, it's impossible to calculate when you are fertile. The rhythm method is like playing pin the tail on the donkey with your birth control. Sure, you could be lucky and blindly happen to find the right spot, but you could also be off, pin the tail on his stomach, and end up pregnant. (One out of four couples who use this method do.)

Another problem with the rhythm method is that sperm can live inside of you for five to seven days. So even if you knew when you were going to be fertile, you wouldn't be able to have sex for a week before that. If for some reason your period is going to come early one month, it would mean that you could get pregnant by having sex while you're still bleeding a little bit from your previous period. It is possible to get pregnant any day of the month because you have no way of knowing exactly when your next period is coming. And having sex without a condom puts you at risk for contracting an STD, no matter where you are in your menstrual cycle.

Side note on sex during your period: As long as you use some form of contraception, and you don't mind the mess, it's fine to have sex during your period. Because of the blood, however, if you have an STD, you may be more likely to pass it on to your partner. So if you're going to have sex while you're on your period, make sure that you use a condom.

EMERGENCY CONTRACEPTION

The one time I had to use emergency contraception, I was really nervous. I thought the pharmacist filling the prescription was going to think I was a careless whore who screwed half the lacrosse team in one night with no protection. Having to use emergency contraception made me feel unprepared and irresponsible. I was so concerned with what the pharmacist was thinking that I ended up nervously explaining "I was having sex and the condom came off . . . which was strange because I do know the right way to put one on . . . and it was my boyfriend, not a random one-night stand . . . I don't want you to think I sleep around or anything." The pharmacist just stared at me like I was crazy—but I'm pretty sure he didn't think I was irresponsible (not that it really would have mattered if he did).

Sometimes, no matter how good you try to be with birth control, something screws up. And that doesn't mean that you're careless or slutty. Luckily, we have the option of emergency contraception—birth control that can be taken after the act of sex. You may want to use emergency contraception if you had unprotected sex, had sex using the "pull and pray" method, had sex using the rhythm method, missed two birth control pills in a row, or had a condom slip off or break (and it was your only form of protection). The sooner you start taking emergency contraception, the better, but you can use it up to *five days* after having unprotected sex. (Please note that emergency contraception can't protect you from any STD that you may have been exposed to by having unprotected sex.)

Many girls are hesitant to use emergency contraception because they think that it's the same as having an abortion. It's not. The difference is that an abortion ends a pregnancy after it has begun. Emergency contraception works the same way as birth control pills and condoms by preventing pregnancy from happening in the first place. There is an "abortion pill," but it is *not* the same thing as emergency contraception. Emergency contraceptive pills have the same hormones as birth control pills, just in much higher concentrations.

A package of emergency contraceptive pills contains two pills: one you take right away, and another you take twelve hours later. The most common side effects that girls experience from taking emergency contraception are nausea and throwing up. Certain kinds of pills—ones that are "progestin only"—are less likely to make you puke (or your doctor can prescribe a pill that will help prevent vomiting). Other possible side effects of taking emergency contraception include dizziness, sore breasts, headaches, and irregular vaginal bleeding. But any side effects should go away within one to two days.

Emergency contraception is easy to obtain, and you don't even have to go to your usual doctor to get it (or tell your parents). If you are sexually active, it's a good idea to keep a dose of emergency contraceptive pills on hand just in case (especially because many girls need them on the weekend—when doctors' offices may be closed). To get emergency contraception, talk to your doctor, or call Planned Parenthood at 1-800-230-PLAN. The operator can give you a list of places in your area where you can get a prescription for it and answer any questions you might have. (Please note that, due to religious beliefs, some pharmacies refuse to fill prescriptions for emergency contraception. This is another reason why it's a good idea to get some even if you don't need it; it may take a while to find a pharmacy that will fill the prescription for you.)

FURTHER INFORMATION ON BIRTH CONTROL

✳ BirthControl.com (information about birth control products): http://www.birthcontrol.com

✳ Coalition for Positive Sexuality (information about birth control): http://www.positive.org/JustSayYes/birthcontrol.html

✳ EC Campaign Toolkit (information about emergency contraception): http://www.backupyourbirthcontrol.org/materials/index .htm

✳ Kids Health Organization (information about birth control in the teen section): http://www.kidshealth.org

✳ "Teen Wire" from Planned Parenthood (information about birth control in the "In Focus" section): http://www.teenwire.com

Chapter 9
Pregnancy
The Big "(Uh)O"

For me, PMS stands for "Pregnancy Maniac Syndrome." After I started having sex, I would spend the week before my period agonizing over whether or not it would actually come, and whether or not I was pregnant. It didn't matter how many kinds of contraception I used. I was always nervous.

In the days before I was supposed to get my period, I would go into full-blown stalker mode, searching for any sign of it. I'd discreetly grab my boobs every couple of hours to see if they were "unusually tender." I'd twist around in my seat to see if I was starting to get cramps. And if I noticed any kind of wetness in my underwear, I'd run to the bathroom and pull off my pants.

As you can imagine, by the day my period was actually supposed to come, it already felt like it was a week late. And I would always be positive that "this month it just wasn't coming."

Then it would come: sometimes right on time, sometimes a little late, and sometimes a lot late. Until one month—it actually didn't come at all. It was a nightmare come true.

I made my boyfriend buy the test because I didn't want to pay ten dollars and confess to a cashier that I might be pregnant. I was so freaked out that, not only did I insist on taking it at my boyfriend's place, but I also actually made him come into the bathroom with me. The toilet in his college apartment was clogged, so in order to take the test, I had to hold on to the grimy shower wall and pee in the bathtub. I squatted down over the drain and peed over both the test and my feet. And all I could say while I waited was, "I'm so scared."

Knowing now that I wasn't actually pregnant, I laugh about the ridiculous scene—a toilet about to overflow with shit water, a nervous boyfriend, and a crying girl tinkling on her toes. At the time, however, it was terrifying.

Worrying about being pregnant sucks. The better you are about using contraception, the less you have to worry. But no matter how careful you are, most sexually active girls have a pregnancy scare eventually, and many will actually be pregnant. According to the National Campaign to Prevent Teen Pregnancy, one out of every three teen girls will become pregnant before she is twenty. This chapter is about figuring out if you are pregnant and, if you are, deciding what to do.

LATE PERIODS

There are many reasons that periods can be late, and, luckily, pregnancy is only one of them. It's normal for girls in their teens and early twenties to have irregular periods, so if your period is late and you're very responsible about using contraception (or aren't sexually active), one of the following reasons could be the cause.

Stress. Going through a stressful time can definitely make your period late. Maybe you've had a lot of work, you just broke up with a boyfriend, you're trying to make an important decision, or you're dealing with a major life change. Anything that has thrown you off mentally can also throw you off physically.

Change in exercise habits. The amount you exercise can also affect your menstrual cycle. Perhaps you just started playing a sport and are exercising more than usual, or maybe you decided you were too busy and stopped exercising altogether. Any drastic changes in your normal pattern of physical activity can make your period come late.

Rapid weight loss or gain. Rapidly losing or gaining considerable amounts of weight puts stress on your body and can disrupt your menstrual cycle. If you have lost a lot of weight, your period is not coming, and you're not pregnant, you should speak with your doctor. When a girl's period stops coming for a reason other than pregnancy, it's a sign that she isn't healthy.

Change of diet. A significant change in diet can also make your period late. Changing your diet means completely switching the types of food you're eating for weeks at a time (not: "Two weeks ago, I was real hungry and ate a whole pizza"). A change in diet may happen if you move, or go on a long vacation (both of which can affect your menstrual cycle, even if your diet has remained the same).

Illness. If you have gotten fairly sick since your last period, it can cause your next period to be late. A small cold should not make a difference, but a major barf-your-brains-out flu might. Any sickness that immobilizes you for several days may disrupt your cycle.

Changes in sleep patterns. Sleeping more or less than usual (which may be a result of feeling stressed out) can make your period come late. If your body is used to getting a certain amount of rest and you change your normal patterns, you may be changing your menstrual patterns as well.

Medication. Starting or stopping the use of medications may affect the timing of your period. Some medications known for disrupting a girl's menstrual cycle include birth control pills, thyroid medications, and antidepressants. If you are taking any kind of prescription pill and are experiencing a late period, you should ask your doctor if menstrual disruptions are a possible side effect of the medication.

Your period may come late for many reasons. Often it's late because something has happened in the previous month that's out of the ordinary. Any type of physical, emotional, or environmental change can affect your menstrual cycle. (If having an unpredictable period is something that bothers you, taking birth control pills will help make it more regular—as well as greatly decrease the chance that you will get pregnant.) While it's normal to be late, completely missing a period is something that you should be concerned about. While it is possible to miss a period and have it mean nothing (even if you are on birth control pills), it can also mean that you are pregnant.

COULD I BE PREGNANT?

The first step to deciding if you could be pregnant is to figure out whether or not you've done anything in the past month that could lead to pregnancy. Although this seems straightforward (either you had sex or you didn't), there actually *are* some gray areas. For the situations that may put you at risk for pregnancy but aren't as clear-cut, see the hookup flow chart below. It might help answer some of your "Could I get pregnant if . . ." questions. (To use this chart, choose one of the four scenarios at the top and work your way down.)

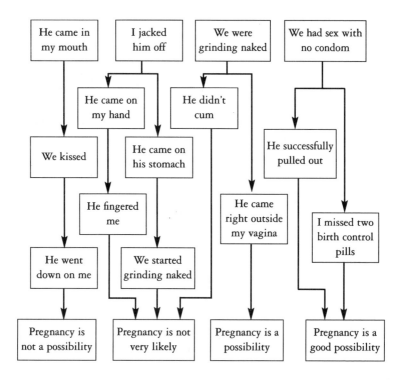

"Create Your Own Hookup Adventure"

If your period is late and there's a possibility that you could be pregnant, you should take a pregnancy test. You should also be on the lookout for any of the telltale signs of pregnancy, such as breast tenderness, nausea (especially in the morning), fatigue, change in appetite, frequent urination, dizziness, or minor cramps (ghost cramps). The confusing thing about the signs of pregnancy is that some of them (like having sore breasts, increased appetite, and minor cramps) can indicate that you're about to get your period.

Many girls who are pregnant experience no warning other than a missed period. So while it's useful to know which signs indicate pregnancy, taking a test is the only definite way of knowing whether or not you are pregnant. If you are over two weeks late, no matter what else you are feeling (or not feeling), take a test.

PREGNANCY TESTS

Getting yourself to take a pregnancy test can be a challenge because there's always that part of you that thinks, "I just don't want to know." And of course, once you take the test, you'll know. But avoiding a pregnancy test isn't going change whether or not you're pregnant. Sure, you could wait four months until you start to grow a belly to finally know for sure, but at that point you'll have far fewer options. If you're pregnant, it's best to find out as soon as possible.

You can buy pregnancy tests at most drugstores for close to ten dollars, and they're generally very reliable. (Most tests claim to be between 97 and 99 percent accurate.) Although it may be your natural reaction to feel uneasy when buying a pregnancy test, it's nothing to be embarrassed or ashamed about; many girls have pregnancy scares. Besides, the store clerk is probably too busy watching the clock or thinking about dinner to care at all about what you're buying. If you're really freaked out about purchasing a pregnancy test, you can always ask a friend (or your partner) to do it for you. Finding out whether you're pregnant is much more important than whatever hesitations you may have about purchasing the test.

There are many different types and brands of pregnancy tests. (And, of course, they all claim to be the most accurate and easiest to use.) The best ones have two windows: one tells you that you performed the test correctly, and the other tells you if you're pregnant. But whatever type of pregnancy test you end up buying, be sure that you read the instructions carefully *before* you use it. One of the most important things to pay attention to is how soon after a missed period you can use the test. If the test says you have to be two weeks late, then make sure that it has actually been two weeks since you were supposed to get your period. If you take a pregnancy test too early, a negative result doesn't mean anything. Because there's always room for error, it's a good idea to take more than one test to make sure that each one gives you the same result. If the tests come back negative and you still aren't getting your period, you should talk to a doctor.

The possibility of being pregnant is very scary, so you may want to have a close friend, your partner, or a parent there with you when you take the test. (You can have them wait for you *outside* the door.) Choose a person who can help you stay calm and will help look into your options if the test comes out positive.

What If I *Am* Pregnant?

An unwanted pregnancy can be both terrifying and frustrating. But as upset as you may be, it's unproductive to beat yourself up over the fact that you're pregnant; there isn't anything you can do to change the past. You need to focus all your energy on deciding your next step. As difficult as dealing with an unplanned pregnancy will be, remember that you are not alone. Each year, thousands of girls become unexpectedly pregnant; this is something that you—like the others—will get through.

Deciding what to do about your pregnancy will be hard. But the sooner you make your decision, the better. You have three choices: have the baby, have the baby and give it up for adoption, or have an abortion. There is no all-encompassing right answer that is going to be the best decision for everyone, and ultimately only *you* can decide what is best given your personal situation.

If I were pregnant, I know that I would want my parents' support. I also know that not everyone feels like they can talk with their parents about sex, and especially about being pregnant. If you truly cannot talk to your parents, you should try talking with another adult that you trust—a relative, a friend's mother, or your doctor. This adult can help you schedule an appointment with a gynecologist to check the status of your pregnancy, as well as help you decide what to do.

Another option is to meet with a counselor at your local Planned Parenthood, who will give you information on having a baby, giving a baby up for adoption, and ending your pregnancy. She will also give you some questions to think about that will help you decide what option is best for you. To locate a Planned Parenthood, or to make an appointment with a counselor, call 1-800-230-PLAN.

CRISIS PREGNANCY CENTERS

If you are pregnant and looking for a clinic where you can discuss your options, be sure that you don't accidentally stumble into a crisis pregnancy center. Crisis pregnancy centers are fake clinics set up by religious fanatics who lure in young pregnant women and try to persuade them not to have an abortion. The staff members at one of these clinics may give you a free pregnancy test, but they may also make you listen to anti-abortion propaganda for an hour or more before they give you the results.

A qualified clinic will give you information about all your pregnancy options and then let *you* decide what is best. Crisis pregnancy centers advertise "free counseling," but the "counselor" may not give you medically accurate information; she will give you information that supports her belief that abortion is a sin. The people who work at crisis pregnancy centers don't care whether you make the decision that is best for you; they only care that you don't have an abortion. They may harass you, try to intimidate you, make you feel guilty, make you pray with them, and perhaps even prevent you from leaving until they're done lecturing you—not what you want if you just found out that you're pregnant. The following are some ways to recognize crisis pregnancy centers.

✳ The clinic is located next to a high school and has one of the telltale names. Crisis pregnancy centers usually bank on the fact that, if a teenage girl gets pregnant, she'll walk into the first clinic she sees. Some of the common names of these centers are "Crisis Pregnancy Center," "Pregnancy Aid," "Birth Right," "Open Door," or "Pregnancy Counseling Center."

✳ The center is listed in the phone book under "abortion alternatives." In some phone books, the center may actually be listed under "abortion." These centers falsely advertise the services they offer so that they can attract women who are thinking about having an abortion and then persuade them to continue with their pregnancy instead.

✳ The center won't tell you anything over the phone. If you are looking for a clinic where you can discuss your pregnancy options, always call first. If the center is legitimate and offers a range of options, you should be able to get information about those services over the phone. When you ask whether the clinic provides (or gives referrals for) abortion services, you should get a straightforward answer. If the center won't tell you much on the phone and keeps urging you to come in, you may have called a pregnancy crisis center.

If you are pregnant, you want to consider all your options. Unfortunately, since abortion is such a political and religious issue, there are many places that may give you false information about abortions so that you won't consider it as an option. There are even Web sites (often with deceptive names) that claim to counsel women on all their pregnancy options, but actually provide only anti-abortion propaganda.

If you want accurate information about your options, it's your safest bet to call your doctor or Planned Parenthood (1-800-230-PLAN) and ask one of them to recommend a reliable clinic. You can also look at the pregnancy page on Planned Parenthood's Web site (www.plannedparenthood .org/pp2/portal/files/portal/medicalinfo/pregnancy/pub-pregnant.xml), which has information about continuing a pregnancy, putting a baby up for adoption, and having an abortion. It also has a list of questions you should consider when deciding which option is best for you.

CONTINUING WITH YOUR PREGNANCY

If there is any chance that you will continue your pregnancy, you will need to quit smoking or drinking immediately (if you do either), refrain from taking any unprescribed drugs, and make an appointment to see your doctor as soon as possible (especially if you take medication regularly). Taking good care of yourself during your pregnancy is very important for the health of your child. Many young mothers aren't fully informed about the health precautions they should take while pregnant, and as a result, their babies are more likely to have health problems. If you see a healthcare provider and follow his or her instructions, you are much more likely to have a healthy baby.

Making the decision to be a young (and perhaps single) mother is a huge commitment. You may want to find some young mothers to talk with about what it's like to have a child when you're young. You may also want to talk with your parents to see if they will help out with the financial aspects of having a baby. Raising a child requires a great deal of money, as well as your constant attention.

If you have a baby, you will have to be prepared to put your child's needs before your own (something that is difficult for many young women to do). This may mean giving up your education, since, according to the National Campaign to Prevent Teen Pregnancy, only a third of teen mothers finish high school, and less than 2 percent get a college degree by the time they're thirty. If you're going to continue your pregnancy, you need to be fully aware of how having a baby will influence the rest of your life.

On the following pages is the story of a woman who decided to become a teenage mother.

MOTHERING: BY H.A.S., 19

Ever since I can remember, I have always wanted a baby. I dreamed of feeling that unconditional love that everyone talks about. As I got older, the feelings got stronger. By the time I was in high school, I was obsessed with babies and anything that had to do with them. Sometimes I would go to the store so that I could look at baby clothes and dream about my future baby. I just felt like having a baby was my calling in life. So after I had been dating my boyfriend for two years, it wasn't exactly an accident that I got pregnant.

My reaction to the pregnancy test wasn't what I had expected it to be. Not only was I nervous and ashamed to tell my family, I found out that I was pregnant the day before my senior trip to the Bahamas. You can imagine how much fun that was. I immediately had my first test of responsibility: no drinking and no partying. As hard as that was, I knew that, no matter what, I could not give up or abort my baby.

I began taking on the full responsibility of keeping my baby healthy. I started taking prenatal vitamins and going to childbirth classes once a week. I quit smoking immediately, started eating healthily, and began watching very carefully what I put in my body. I became much more aware of my environment to the point where I wouldn't watch scary movies or listen to loud music so that it wouldn't affect my baby. Most of the time, I wouldn't even go in places like pool halls because of the smoke. And, after nine months, I finally gave birth to my beautiful baby boy.

I can remember countless people telling me that raising a baby is much harder than you think. You never get a moment to yourself, and, most of all, you can't ever give the baby back. My response was always, "Don't worry, I love babies. I'll be fine. I've baby-sat plenty of them!" Well, I found out the hard way.

I think many teenagers are misled about the time and energy it takes to raise a child. When you fully take on the responsibility of raising a child, you also have to realize that it's the end of sleep at night, the end of going out, and the end of being able to do something as simple as taking a shower or going to the bathroom without a baby either sitting on your lap or screaming in the other room. It is much different to hear about these things than to experience them. Trust me. Imagine having to give up your own life for another and having to put that person's needs before your wants for the rest of your life! I have also gotten to experience great things, like my son's first smile, first steps, and first laugh, but it has been tough.

Anyone who is pregnant and is thinking about having a baby needs to be aware that it's not fair to the baby if you're not ready to give up your life, devote all your time to your baby, and make decisions based on what is the healthiest for your baby. I also want to say that I love my son to death, and I wouldn't give him up for the world, but if I had to go back, I would wait until I got my life together and my future settled. My son and I are doing great now, but I know that these few months are just the beginning. Hard times will come in the future, but fun times will come as well. Having a baby is a wonderful experience of patience and love.

FACTS ABOUT TEEN MOTHERS
According to the National Campaign to Prevent Teen Pregnancy

* More than 50 percent of teen mothers expect that they will marry the father of their baby.

* Only 8 percent actually do.

* Over 80 percent of teen mothers end up on welfare.

* Only 30 percent receive child support payments from the father of their child.

ADOPTION

If raising a child is not something you are prepared to do, and having an abortion is not an option for you either, you may decide that adoption is best for you and the baby. Babies can be put up for adoption through agencies (that find parents for your baby) or independently (by finding parents on your own). If you are considering adoption, these are some things you may want to consider.

You will go through nine months of pregnancy and childbirth, and then your baby will be taken away. Some women find the thought of being separated from their baby very painful, even if they know that they can't take on the responsibility of starting a family. Others find comfort in the idea of putting their baby into a home that is better prepared to raise a child.

You may never see your child or know how he or she is doing. In some types of adoption, you can choose to know the names of the parents who are taking your baby and maintain contact with them. In other types of adoption, you will never know the name of the family, and they will never know your name either. Either type you choose, your baby will belong to other people, and you will not have a significant presence (if any) in your child's life.

You can't change your mind later. Although adoption laws vary state by state, you will sign adoption papers soon after your child is born and have a very short time to change your mind. Even if you are tempted to change your mind and keep the baby, remember that you chose adoption for a reason: you weren't prepared to raise a child.

Giving a child up for adoption is undoubtedly difficult. According to the National Committee for Adoption, only two or three out of every hundred pregnant teens decide to do it. But the ones who do choose adoption do so because the idea of being separated from their baby is less painful than the idea of not having the baby at all. Many girls who have put a child up for adoption are comforted by knowing that they gave a child to a couple who otherwise would not have been able to raise children (or to a couple who has always wanted to adopt).

Recently, a teenage girl who was adopted told me, "Putting me up for adoption was the best way that my mother could say, 'I love you.' She wanted me to have a better life than what she could offer me. My mother knew that by giving me up, I would become part of a family that had the time and money to raise a child and that I would have better opportunities."

ABORTION

If you are pregnant and do not want to continue a pregnancy, you can choose to have an abortion. Most girls who decide to have an abortion do so because they can't afford to have a baby, they don't feel mature enough to have a baby, and they don't want to mold their daily schedule and future plans around a baby.

If you want to have an abortion, you will have to decide within the first twenty-three weeks of being pregnant (and even sooner in some states). Most young women who have an abortion do so within the first twelve weeks. The earlier you decide to have an abortion, the safer it is, and the less it costs. According to Planned Parenthood, as long as you go to a qualified clinic, having an abortion actually has fewer risks than going through childbirth. A correctly performed abortion should not affect a woman's physical health or her ability to have children in the future.

There are three types of abortions: medical abortions, vacuum aspirations, and surgical abortions. If you decide to have an abortion within the first nine weeks of being pregnant, you can have a medical abortion. During a medical abortion, you are given medicine that will cause you to miscarry (basically get a very heavy period). Vacuum aspirations can be performed within the first fourteen weeks of pregnancy. During this procedure (performed at a clinic), a long tube will be inserted through the vagina and into the uterus to suck out the fertilized egg. Most women who have had either a medical abortion or a vacuum aspiration say that it feels like severe cramps. Surgical abortions are more invasive procedures and are generally performed in pregnancies further along.

Most young women who are considering having an abortion want to talk with their partner and their parents. However, your partner doesn't *have* to know, and in some states, your parents don't either. (Although if you *can* tell your parents, it's probably a good idea.) Many states require that any girl under eighteen tell her parents she is planning on having an abortion, and some states require that she get her parents' permission. In cases where a girl believes that she truly cannot tell her parents (and the state requires it), she can go in front of a judge who will decide if she is mature enough to make the decision on her own.

If you are considering having an abortion, regardless of who else you wish to talk to about your pregnancy, you can see a counselor at any Planned Parenthood who will help you sort through your options. This counselor will keep your meeting confidential and can inform you about the parental involvement laws in your state and the type of abortion that would be best for you.

According to the Alan Guttmacher Institute, a third of all women have an abortion by the time they are forty-five. So if you want to talk with someone about the experience of having abortion, it won't be difficult to find a woman who can give you firsthand advice. If you do decide to have an abortion, make sure that you have a support system in place, be it your parents, your partner, or a trusted relative or friend.

HAVING AN ABORTION: BY A.E.K., 29

Even if you think you are really smart, are totally responsible, make good choices, and are the type of girl that nothing bad ever happens to, well, sex can make you stupid. At least that's what I learned early on in my dating life. I thought I was the most responsible person around—I didn't do drugs, I didn't drink, I didn't fail out of school, I didn't disobey my parents. But what I did do was have unprotected sex, and it was one of the biggest mistakes of my life.

Self-esteem is a funny thing. If you don't have much of it, then sex can be a minefield where even the most well-meaning person can screw up. For me, the danger lay in having sex with an older man (six years my senior). He was someone whom I looked up to and whom I thought knew so much more about sex than I did. So when he told me that if he "pulled out" before he came I wouldn't get pregnant (I wasn't even thinking about STDs), I believed him—almost. An annoying little voice inside my head kept saying, "Are you sure?" And, "That's not what I heard." But I didn't listen to it because I wanted him to like me.

Twenty-five days later, after the guy had decided to move to Arizona, I found myself alone, without my period, and with a funny feeling in my stomach, like nausea. I couldn't believe that I could possibly be pregnant. I had sex with him only once! But when I took a pregnancy test, there it was, loud and clear.

What did I do? Well, first, I cried a lot. Then I told some friends who were really understanding and helped me feel a little less tormented. After a few days of intense thinking (and talking with various people, including the guy, who came back from Arizona to help me in any way he could), I decided not to have the baby. It was a hard decision, but this time I listened to the voice in my head; it was telling me that I didn't want a baby right now. I couldn't take care of myself at all; how could I take care of a baby, too?

Because it was very early in the pregnancy, I was able to have a "medical abortion," meaning that I got a shot, and then a few days later, in the comfort of my own home, inserted a suppository into my vagina that induced a miscarriage. The physical pain was horrible. (I almost passed out because it hurt so much.) The emotional pain was worse. And when it was over, I knew that I had to make some big changes in my life. I told my parents what had happened. (And though I was worried that they wouldn't love me anymore, they still did.) I got several STD tests, and, thank God, I was disease free. I started seeing a counselor who helped me understand some of the reasons why that event happened: I didn't value myself, and I didn't consider what I felt or thought to be important. It took a while, but I did eventually forgive myself for my mistake. And although I didn't have sex again for several years, I realized that there is nothing wrong with having sex. But there is something wrong with having sex when you know inside that it's not right for you.

Now, five years later, I understand that if I had made a different choice—to have a baby—it wouldn't have been the end of the world for me. But, looking back on it, I don't regret the decision I made. If I had had a baby, I would be in a vastly different place from where I am now. And I really like where I am now—feeling healthy and happy and enjoying a career path that I am passionate about and a relationship with a man who truly loves me (because I love myself!).

I don't regret the mistake I made either because we all make mistakes. But I made sure to learn from mine and to make changes in my life that would lead to making better choices. Choices that would not result in an unwanted pregnancy or an STD.

Someday, I do hope to have a baby, when the time is right for me, and for the person I am with. Until that day, I will never have unprotected sex. I learned the hard way. And, take it from me, in this case, the hard way sucks! I only wish I had someone to tell me that from the beginning. Maybe, if I had, I would have made better choices. Hopefully, you will.

FOR FURTHER INFORMATION AND SUPPORT

* Adopting.org (information about adoption): http://www .adoption.org

* Childbirth.org (information on having a baby): http://www .childbirth.org

* Feminist Women's Health Center (information on having an abortion): http://www.fwhc.org/ab.htm

* Planned Parenthood (general information): http://www.planned parenthood.org

Chapter 10

Sexual Assault

Rape, Rapists, and Recovery

I never spent much time thinking about rape as I was growing up. Like most people, I thought of rape as one scenario: a stranger with a weapon in a dark alley. I thought rapists were sketchy-looking men who drove vans with no windows and raped women because they couldn't get any action. I didn't think that rapes were that common, and I thought that, as long as you were responsible, rape wasn't something to worry about.

Then, I started finding out about girls I knew who had been raped: at a wedding, in a bathroom, at a party, at someone's house. Not one of their assaults fit into my scenario. Nearly everything I thought I knew about rape was false.

The truth is, the majority of rapes happen in places we usually think of as "safe," by perpetrators who seemed like they could be trusted. Rapists can be nice looking, successful, and educated men who have no trouble getting girls. According to the National Violence against Women Survey, more than one out of every six women is a rape victim, and the majority of those victims were assaulted in their teens or early twenties.

Because sexual assaults are so common, as young women, we need to be educated about rape. If we're not, rapists get away with their crimes because the girls they attacked weren't taught exactly what "counts" as rape; rape victims get told that "it wasn't rape" by friends who can't recognize assaults that don't fit into their stereotypical scenario; and, worst of all, victims believe that being raped was their own fault.

This chapter is the truth about rape, rapists, and recovery.

WHAT IS RAPE AND SEXUAL ASSAULT?

The definitions of sexual assault and rape are not as straightforward as many people believe. Many attacks fall into a gray area—where, for one reason or another, the victim may not be sure that what she experienced was in fact a sexual assault. If a victim doesn't know that she has been sexually assaulted, she won't get help, and she may feel partly responsible for what happened to her. For this reason, it's important to be able to recognize all kinds of sexual assaults and rapes, especially those that are less obviously an attack.

Most girls don't know that many of those obnoxious sexual advances they have to deal with "just 'cause they're girls" can actually be sexual assaults. The US Department of Justice defines sexual assault as any kind of unwanted sexual contact. This includes someone grabbing your butt as you walk down the hall, grabbing your breasts when you're sitting on the bus, or forcing your hands down his pants. If anyone without permission grabs or fondles your breasts, butt, or genitalia, or forces you to touch his, it is sexual assault (no matter how quickly the incident may be over).

Rape is a more severe form of sexual assault—defined as forced vaginal, anal, or oral penetration. "Forced" includes psychological force (such as verbal threats) as well as physical force. And the penetrating article can be a penis, a tongue, a finger, or even a bottle or another object. The term *rape* describes many different scenarios, not the least of which is a stranger physically forcing himself onto a girl. All of the following situations "count" as rape.

✳ *A friend, boyfriend, ex-boyfriend, or anyone a girl has slept with in the past made her have sex when she didn't want to.* Just because a girl had sex with a guy once (or even hundreds of times), it does not give him the go-ahead to have sex with her *whenever* he feels like it. If a girl tells her boyfriend that she doesn't want to have sex, it is rape if he forces her.

✳ *A girl was forced into sex by a guy whom she had sex with willingly at a later time.* If a girl was raped by a guy and then willingly had sex with him later, it doesn't make the rape "not count." Although this may seem like a bizarre scenario, there are many reasons it could happen. It probably happens most commonly when a girl is raped by someone she cares about (perhaps a boyfriend). Even though she knows that he has raped her, she may forgive him and end up having sex with him in the future. Another possibility is that a girl doesn't recognize that what happened to her was rape and, as a result, sleeps with the perpetrator at some point after the incident. (She may see it as, "Well, I've already slept with him once, why not?")

✳ *A girl had sex but was too drunk, high, or young to understand what she was doing.* A girl can consent to sex only if she truly understands what is happening. Even if a seven-year-old doesn't explicitly say no to a teenaged guy having sex with her, it still counts as rape because there's no way that a girl that young can be expected to fully grasp what's going on. On the same note, if a guy has sex with a girl who is too messed up on drugs or alcohol to know what's she's doing, then it's not sex; it's rape.

✳ *A guy forced a girl to have sex with him but told her that he loved her, that she was beautiful, or that she was so sexy he couldn't control himself.* A rapist may be "nice" to a girl he rapes either during the incident or after it is over. But regardless of how a perpetrator may flatter a girl, if he forced her into sex, what happened is still rape. Even if a guy *is* truly in love with a girl, it doesn't mean that he cannot rape her. "Love" doesn't turn rape into consensual sex.

✳ *A girl was forced into having sex, but her body responded and she "got wet" or even had an orgasm.* A rapist may try to convince a victim that an act was not rape by telling her that she "wanted it" because while he was raping her she got wet. But even if a girl did get wet, and even if she had an orgasm, if she was forced to have sex, it is rape. Female bodies are designed to respond to sexual stimulation—even sometimes unwanted stimulation.

✳ *A guy threatened to harm a girl if she didn't have sex with him, so she did it because she felt forced.* If a guy threatens to hurt or blackmail a girl unless she has sex with him, he is raping her by using psychological intimidation or threat of force. Even if she agrees to have sex with him, it still counts as rape because saying no wasn't an option.

Anytime that anyone (be it a relative, boyfriend, friend, stranger, date, or teacher) forces you in any way (physically or psychologically) to have sex (digital, oral, anal, or vaginal), it "counts" as rape.

RAPISTS

One of the biggest misconceptions about rape is that rapists are strangers lurking in dark alleys, behind bushes, or in sleazy bars. Most people's vision of a rapist is a greasy, snaggle-toothed man whom no one would ever be attracted to. Many believe that a man rapes because he's desperate and it's the only way he can get sex. But this is not the case at all.

According to the National Crime and Victimization Survey, 66 percent of all rape victims know their attacker, and in victims under eighteen, when all sexual assaults are included, 93 percent know their attacker. In fact, according to the Sex Offenses and Offenders study, half of all sexual assaults take place in either the victim's home or the house of a friend, neighbor, or relative. Although some of the men who sexually assault are strangers, the majority are acquaintances, relatives, partners, and "friends."

There's no way to spot a rapist just by looking at him. They aren't just men who are "too gross to get any." Some are attractive, successful, charming, athletic, and rich. Some are even married. Sexual assaults happen because a man wants to control a woman, not because it is the only way he can get sex. Sexual assault experts agree that rape is a crime motivated by power, not sex.

WHAT COUNTS AS NO?

Many sexual assault victims aren't sure if they were assaulted because they don't know if how they responded during their rape was a clear enough indication of no. As a result, many victims feel responsible for being raped because they feel that they could have said "stop" more times, more firmly. There are many ways a girl can verbally or physically indicate that she doesn't want to have sex, and once she does, it is a guy's responsibility to listen to her—if he doesn't, it is rape. All these following scenarios "count" as ways of saying no.

* ✳ *A girl said no but didn't physically fight off her attacker.* A girl saying that she doesn't want to have sex is enough for a guy to understand that he needs to stop. Girls shouldn't have to physically fight off sex if they don't want it. And the reality is, even if a girl does attempt to fight off her attacker, it often doesn't make a difference because men are generally much stronger than women.

* ✳ *A girl said yes at first, then changed her mind and said no.* Even if a girl starts hooking up with a guy willingly, she still has the right to tell him to stop if things start going too far. Initially agreeing to a sexual encounter doesn't make "no" any less meaningful—it still means no.

* ✳ *A girl didn't say no because she was afraid that she would be physically hurt or killed if she did.* If a rapist is using a weapon or extreme physical force, a girl may never say no or resist an attack because she is afraid for her safety. At the time a girl is raped, she has to concentrate on surviving the attack and, in some situations, that may mean not saying or doing anything.

✳ *A girl stopped saying no because it wasn't making the guy stop.* If a girl says that she doesn't want to have sex, she doesn't have to say it more than once for the guy to understand. If he isn't listening to her and isn't stopping, the girl may stop saying no—but that doesn't count as yes.

✳ *A girl showed pain or fear, and obviously didn't want the sexual encounter to continue.* If a girl shows clear physical signs that she doesn't want to be engaging in a sex act, then, even if she doesn't verbally tell a guy to stop, her actions clearly mean, "No. I don't want this."

✳ *A girl never said no because she froze up and said nothing.* Some rape victims are so shocked and scared while they are being raped that they literally can't move or speak. Although technically a girl may have never said, "I don't want to have sex," if she is showing no signs that she *wants* to have sex, then her actions don't mean yes—they mean no.

Any way that a girl says no or "stop" means that a guy needs to stop. And if a girl isn't responding in any way, her lack of any response doesn't mean yes. It is a guy's responsibility to stop a sexual encounter at the first sign that a girl does not want it to happen. If he ignores those signs, it is rape.

It can be difficult for a girl to comprehend that she was raped, especially if the perpetrator was an acquaintance or a friend. Some victims assume that how they acted "wasn't a clear enough no," because if it was, the guy would have stopped—this can be easier than believing that a friend or boyfriend knowingly raped them. As difficult as it can be to fathom that a guy would knowingly force a girl into sex, it happens. And when it does, it is always the fault of a guy for not stopping rather than a girl for not being able to make him stop. When a girl verbally or physically says no, no matter how timidly it was said or acted, it means no.

IMPORTANT: WHAT TO DO IF YOU HAVE BEEN RAPED

If you have been raped, the first thing you need to do is get to a safe place. The place should be away from the attacker, and somewhere that he can't easily find you. This may be the house of a friend, relative, or neighbor who will believe you and be able to get you immediate help. Once you are safe, follow these steps.

1. Do not shower, bathe, or brush your teeth, and, if you can hold it, don't go to the bathroom. Although your first instinct may be to clean yourself off, doing this can destroy evidence that you may need if you decide to press charges. It's best not to change clothes; but if you have already taken them off, put them in a clean *paper* bag. Write down any specific details of the attack while they are still fresh in your mind.

2. Call the National Sexual Assault Hotline (available twenty-four hours a day) at 1-800-656-HOPE. The counselor on the line will be able to talk you through what steps you should take next and refer you to a local rape crisis center. Calling this hotline *does not* mean that you are reporting the rape to the police. Even if you're not sure that you want to press charges or formally report the rape to police, it's important that you get the medical attention you need.

3. Get prompt medical attention. If you cannot use a phone, or you don't have the number of the sexual assault hotline, you can go directly to an emergency room. Once you are there, you should ask whether there is a Sexual Assault Nurse Examiner (SANE nurse) available. Although you can see any doctor or nurse, SANE nurses have been specially trained to treat victims of sexual assault.

   Even if you don't think that you've been physically injured, it's important to see a doctor after a rape. A doctor can help you take preventive measures against pregnancy and STDs. If you want to decrease your chances of pregnancy, you will need to take emergency contraception within five days of the rape (but the sooner you take it, the better). And if you believe that you have been exposed to HIV, there are drugs you can take within thirty-six hours of the attack that will decrease the likelihood of transmission.

4. Ask for a rape-kit exam. When you are at the hospital, you should have a rape-kit exam. Although this exam can feel very invasive, it will collect evidence that will be necessary if you decide to press charges against your attacker. Once the evidence is collected, it is held confidentially, and if you decide that you don't want to press charges against your attacker, the evidence is thrown away. Having the rape-kit exam does not mean that you have to press charges; it just means that the evidence is available *if* you decide to take legal action. According to the US Department of Justice, the chances of getting a rapist convicted are significantly higher if a rape-kit exam is performed. *Important:* It is best to have a rape-kit exam as soon as possible after the attack, but you can have one performed as long as five days afterward.

5. It's never too late to get help. Even if you have been assaulted years ago, it's not too late to get counseling. Many victims don't end up getting help until months or years later, but then lead much happier lives after they do. Even if your needs aren't urgent, you can still call the sexual assault hotline.

KEEPING YOURSELF SAFE

Although you may not be able to protect yourself completely from a sexual assault, you can take measures to reduce your risk of being assaulted. As a general rule, when you go out, try to stick with a group of friends. Be discriminating about who you go off alone with; if you start to feel uneasy or uncomfortable, make up an excuse to leave. ("I have to run to the bathroom" is usually a good one.) If you know ahead of time that you're going to be out with a guy you don't know very well, give either your parents or a friend his full name, cell phone number, and address if you have it. It's always a good idea to have someone know where you are at all times.

Whenever you're at a party, club, or bar, never leave eyeshot of your drink or accept one that is open. If someone offers me an open drink, I always say, "No, thanks, I'm a germ-a-phobe—I can't take open drinks because I always think someone has spit in it." Sure, it sounds a little funny, but it's better than accusing a guy of attempting to drug me, or risking being drugged. Substances like GHB, Ketamine (K) and Rohypnol (roofies) can be slipped very discreetly into drinks, and, since they won't change the color or taste of the drink, you won't know it was given to you until you start to feel very intoxicated. If you ever start to feel strange or too drunk based on what you had to drink, find a friend or someone you trust immediately. Make sure that he or she removes you from the potentially dangerous situation and gets you medical attention. Trust your instincts, and even if you fear that a guy will think you're rude or crazy, if you feel unsafe, get away.

When you're hooking up with a guy, tell him how far you want to go in the beginning. That way, there's no confusion about what's OK and what isn't. It doesn't have to be a drawn-out negotiation—just briefly mention, "Just so you know, I don't want to . . ." Remember that the responsibility to respect your limits falls on him. If he pushes you further than you want to go, it is his fault for not listening to you, not your fault for "not being clear."

RAPE IS NEVER YOUR FAULT

Many victims feel responsible for their sexual assault because they think that they could have been more careful or somehow prevented it. But being sexually assaulted or raped is never the victim's fault.

The reality is, just by living a "normal, everyday life," you're putting yourself at risk for rape, injury, and even death. Every time you get into a car, there is a chance that you'll be hit by another driver. But if that happens, no one would say that the accident was your fault because you made the "irresponsible decision" of being in an automobile. Girls get raped in situations that other girls are in every day without any consequence. You can't be expected to never put yourself in the presence of men because one of them might rape you, just like you can't be expected to never get into a car so that you won't have an accident. A girl isn't responsible for being raped because she agreed to go on a date with a guy, went off alone with a guy, or started to hook up with a guy—doing that is a part of life.

Rape is something that someone else does to you, and you cannot be held accountable for another person's actions. What someone does to you against your will is out of your control. Regardless of what situation you put yourself in, what you were wearing, what you had to drink, or how you said no, being raped is never your fault.

COMING FORWARD

Many victims don't tell anyone that they were sexually assaulted, or, if they do, it isn't until a long time after it happened. Some victims keep their rape a secret because they're ashamed of what happened or believe that it's their own fault. Others stay quiet because they think that rape is a personal problem they should deal with on their own. And some don't tell because they're afraid that no one will believe them.

As personal as an assault may feel, it's not a problem you should keep to yourself (even if the guy who raped you was your boyfriend). Many girls who have been sexually assaulted end up dependent on drugs or alcohol; many also develop Post-Traumatic Stress Disorder (PTSD). (The main signs of PTSD are persistent avoidance of places or things that are reminders of the rape; constantly reliving the rape through nightmares or flashbacks; feeling detached from other people; feeling anxious, angry, jumpy; and having trouble sleeping.) Rape survivors who seek counseling are more likely to confront their feelings, and less likely to experience the negative health consequences that can result from a sexual assault.

If you have been raped, it's likely affecting both your physical and mental health. You shouldn't hesitate to speak with a counselor or a therapist, especially if you are experiencing symptoms of PTSD, or if you have begun to use drugs or alcohol heavily. Even if you never want to tell anyone you know about the rape (or you're afraid that no one you know will believe you), you can get help privately by calling the National Sexual Assault Hotline (1-800-656-HOPE) or going to your local rape crisis center.

Opening up about a rape or sexual assault is your own decision. But as difficult as it may be, nearly all victims who have gotten help have found that step vital to healing and getting on with their lives. If you are struggling with whether to tell someone about a past sexual assault, you may find it helpful to speak with other women who are in your position. There are many online chat rooms where you can find other rape survivors—a popular site is Pandora's Aquarium (http://pandys.org). Whom you tell about your sexual assault is your business, but often, finding someone to talk with is the first step to healing.

IF A FRIEND IS ASSAULTED

If a friend of yours has been sexually assaulted, the best thing that you can do is to listen and believe her. When she tells you her story, give her the benefit of the doubt; don't judge her actions, and don't tell her she should have done something differently. If she has just been assaulted, encourage her to call the National Sexual Assault Hotline and to seek medical attention.

Be sure that you support your friend, not only the day after, but also the week, month, and year after. A friend of mine who was raped said that the hardest thing for her was that, after the first week, everyone acted like she should "just get over it." If your friend has been sexually assaulted, it may take her a while to heal, and she'll need any support you can give her throughout the entire process.

The following is one girl's story about her experience with a sexual assault and how she came forward.

UNTITLED: BY ARIEL WHITE, 17

On July 22, I will celebrate my eighteenth birthday, as well as my fifth. I say this because it will be five years since my first life ended, and five years since my second life began. It has been five years since I was raped. At the age of thirteen, I was still very young and just beginning to become aware of how much attention I received from boys. I loved it. Every summer, my family and I would spend our time in Martha's Vineyard. I spent my days with friends at the beach and in town, searching for my next crush. I had one particular friend whose two good-looking older brothers had surprisingly taken a great interest in me. I craved the attention, amazed that any older guy would even look twice at me. So inclined to be liked and desired, I accepted her oldest brother's plea to walk him to his car one night after a party. Only a minute later I found myself in his truck. My underwear on the floor seemed so distant. He asked and I said no, embarrassed that the words even escaped my mouth. Over and over I said the word "no." But he didn't stop, and I fell into a passive silence. With my eyes fixed on the police station, my body went numb. He finished with glory, putting another trophy on his shelf. He had taken my innocence, my childhood, and my soul.

Walking me back into town, he held my hand as if he knew I was going to collapse if he didn't. Waiting for my friends, tears ran down my face, drowning my feelings. Was I pregnant? Did I have AIDS? All I knew was that I was a disgrace to my family; I was a dirty slut, a good-for-nothing thirteen-year-old whore. But at least I had felt desired. At the time, I believed that if someone had wanted me so badly as to force me to have sex with him, I must have been worth something. As one of my friends approached me, I sighed in relief. Throwing my arms around her for support, I received anything but what I had asked for. She commented in disgust, confirming my fear that I was a disgrace, a disgusting slut.

I continued through freshman year in high school as if nothing had happened. I wasn't apparently different from the outside, only internally. I remember spending most of my time in the girls' bathroom crying, unaware of why, and blaming my hormones. Forgetting entirely about what had happened that previous summer, I became very interested in my appearance and boys. In tenth grade, I transferred to a large public school. I went to every party and fooled around with older guys, jumping at every opportunity to receive attention, feeling as though it would fix my problems. From boyfriend to boyfriend, I continually felt used and worthless. Depressed and afraid of losing all control, I eased my pain with drugs and developed a reputation as well as a habit. I spent my days high on methylphenidates, painkillers, and marijuana. I was treating myself as my rapist had, a worthless object. I believed that if I had enough sex, I would conquer the violent sexual acts committed against me, gaining power over what I felt was spinning out of my control.

With recurring dreams and thoughts of what had happened the summer before freshman year, I began to write about it, thinking that if my memories were transferred onto paper, they would disappear. Leaving my writing scattered around the house as cries for help, my mother came across one and confronted me about it. I was so angry with her for reading it, but that was the very thing that I had wanted. She asked me the age of the boy I wrote about. When I told her, she trembled, explaining to me that I was raped. I agreed as if I knew all along, but I didn't really believe it. I was convinced I could have stopped it; I was convinced that it was my fault.

I have now been in therapy for three years and have come a long way. Although I sometimes still blame myself, thinking that if I hadn't done this or that . . . in the end, nothing gives a young man an excuse to have sex with a little girl. At such a young age, children still look to adults for the right answers, to let them know right from wrong. When you live in a society where you are raised to trust adults, your entire world collapses when you are shown the opposite. Who is there left to trust— can you even trust yourself?

Even through all my pain and struggles, I have also found joy. I was forced to face reality well before I was ready to. I felt dead and alone. Although in a sense I had to start my life over, I was able to begin with new wisdom and insight into myself. I have found myself before any of my fellow peers; I know who I am and what I want.

The hardest thing for me was to get help, and although I didn't do it directly, something inside me knew I needed it. In a society where rape is often misunderstood as consensual sex, it is no wonder that victims feel ashamed and guilty of the crime. Victims of sexual violence are made to believe that it couldn't be anyone's fault but their own, keeping them from realizing that what they experienced was rape.

After all I have been through, I only have one regret, and it is not that I agreed to walk to a guy's car or that I didn't fight harder. I know now that it is not my fault and that saying no once should have been enough. My regret is that I didn't get help earlier. I know that my recovery process would have been much easier if I was aware and educated about rape and if I wasn't afraid or ashamed to speak up. As frightening as it is to come forward, it is much more frightening to deal with the pain on your own. Not getting help may seem like the easy way out, but the longer you hold on to such a painful secret, the longer it will take to gain back control of your life and to be happy.

FURTHER INFORMATION AND STORIES

* Aphrodite Wounded (information for women sexually assaulted by their partners): http://www.pandys.org/aphroditewounded

* Feminist Majority Information (list of resources): http://www.feminist.org/911/assaultlinks.html

* RAINN: Rape, Abuse and Incest National Network (information about rape and sexual assault): http://www.rainn.org

* Scarleteen: Crisis Hotline (information about rape): http://www.scarleteen.com/crisis/index.html

* Welcome to Barbados (information and stories of survivors, as well as other links): http://www.welcometobarbados.org

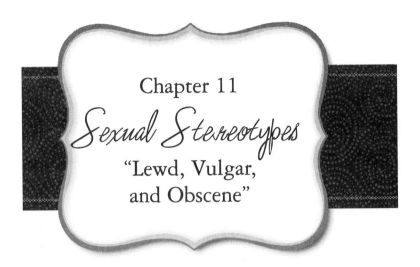

Chapter 11

Sexual Stereotypes

"Lewd, Vulgar, and Obscene"

*S*ex has always scared the shit out of me. I had boobs by the time I was thirteen and, all of a sudden, everything I did and wore seemed sexual. I assumed that since other people saw me as a "sexual being," I was supposed to look and act sexy, and that I had no business trying to be intelligent. This idea was only made worse when my guy friends started commenting on my boobs and telling me I was dumb at around the same time. I started to get really nervous about talking in class because I felt like anything I had to say was probably stupid. And even though I was OK with looking sexy, I felt really dirty and uncomfortable with the whole idea of being sexually intimate with someone. Although I couldn't articulate it at the time, I was dealing with what it means in our society to be a young woman and to be sexual.

Sex and sexuality can come with a lot of emotional baggage when you're a girl. Our culture has some really crappy ideas about female sexuality, and being exposed to and confronted with them is unavoidable. Sexual stereotypes can affect the way you see yourself, the choices you make, and the way you judge other girls. Learning to recognize the stereotypes that define women's sexuality minimizes the effect that they have on your life.

Some of the stereotypes listed in this chapter may seem obvious, cliché, or extreme. But when they present themselves in real life, they are often in messages or actions that are subtle—subtle enough that you fall into believing them without even realizing it. You may be surprised to find that some of these stereotypes seem like facts, which goes to show how ingrained these ideas really are. This chapter is about sexual stereotypes: how to recognize them and how to reject them.

MENSTRUATION IS DIRTY AND DISGUSTING

A stereotype that our culture has a tough time getting over is the notion that the way a girl's reproductive system works is gross. Sure, bodily functions can be kinda nasty in general, but no one seems that concerned about "how disgusting it is" that men ejaculate. Most guys don't freak out about repulsing a girl with their cum. And most girls aren't disturbed by the sight of an unused condom because it makes them think about semen.

Meanwhile, open up any teen magazine to the embarrassing "why me?" story page, and probably half the stories involve a girl's period and a hot guy. There is something about a tampon that we find so embarrassing that we smuggle them into the bathroom down a sock, up a sleeve, or in a purse. Girls are taught that menstruating is disgusting and that we should hide all signs of it from guys. But really, why should guys get so grossed out by something as common as a period? I like to think of it this way.

The majority of guys love vaginas. In fact, they probably spend a good portion of their lives obsessing over them—talking about the ghosts of vaginas past, present, and future. The ones they've been in, the ones they're getting in, and the ones they will never get within five hundred feet of.

On a separate note, most guys love gore: boxing, Arnold Schwarzenegger movies, bloody video games, and any type of extreme sports video where someone gets hurt. You name it, if it's bleeding, it's awesome. Awesome, of course, unless it's a vagina.

So why is it that you can take two things the general male population loves and, when you put them together, they become so "gross"?

The widely accepted idea that periods are disgusting comes from the sentiment that women's vaginas are dirty. Think about it: if a girl skinned her knee and it was gushing blood, it wouldn't be embarrassing. She wouldn't be concerned about a guy seeing her walk into the bathroom with a bandage to stop the flow. (And most likely, a guy would bust his ass to help her, just to show her how "sensitive" he can be). The disturbing thing about menstruation isn't the blood itself—it's the fact that the blood is coming out of a vagina.

The only reason that guys (and girls, for that matter) are grossed out by menstruation is because we have been trained that we should be. But just because we're *taught* that menstrual blood is disgusting, it doesn't mean that we have to buy into it. If we stopped acting like our periods were revolting, guys would stop seeing them that way. Imagine if girls went around bragging about how awesome it is to bleed. Guys would be jealous that their genitals don't do the same thing.

You don't have to absolutely love the fact that you bleed every month, but you don't have to feel ashamed about it either. Menstruation is the sign that we have the ability to carry another life inside of us for nine months, and that's not embarrassing, disgusting, or dirty.

THERE ARE "GOOD GIRLS" AND "BAD GIRLS"

Stereotypically, sexuality divides girls into two categories: the "good girls" and the "bad girls." The "good girls" are the respectable ones who guys want as their girlfriends—the real "bring home to Mom" types. They're innocent, sexually inexperienced, and passive. They don't talk about sex, they don't "get horny," and when they have sex, it's for emotional intimacy, not carnal desire.

Then there are the "bad girls," the ones who guys lust after; the seductresses who wear short skirts and spike heels. They're knowledgeable about sex and in touch with their sexual desires. They're irresistibly sexy, but when it comes to being a guy's girlfriend or wife, they're too impure too pass the test. Take, for example, a *Playboy* model. Would a guy have sex with a woman who poses naked and seductively for a magazine? Probably. Would a guy want that type of girl to bear his children? Probably not.

When the idea of the "good girl" and the "bad girl" play out in reality, it results in girls thinking that guys can either want them sexually or respect them as a person, but not both. It can make girls feel that there is something dirty and disrespectful about sex and they shouldn't express their sexual desires. And it can make girls believe that they have to remain a virgin in order to be "pure" and worthy of respect.

Girls shouldn't use sex as a way to get guys to care about them, but they shouldn't use their virginity in that way either. There is absolutely nothing wrong with a girl not wanting to have sex. At the same time, it's not fair for a girl to get bullied out of sex by hearing, "Guys won't respect you if you do," "Everyone will think you're a slut," or "Sex will be all a guy will want from you." One day, that girl probably will have sex, and when she does, she'll feel horrible about it.

Sex should be something that girls can desire and take pleasure in, not something that makes them feel degraded. Having sex does not make you used up, worthy of disrespect, or incapable of being a nurturing and loving partner. As long as you always respect yourself and engage in sex acts safely and responsibly, there is nothing "bad" about being sexual. You have the same right to enjoy sex as guys do.

GIRLS ARE EITHER SMART OR SEXY

In eleventh grade, I placed within the top ten in my class and as an honor was named a "junior marshal" to help out with the many graduation ceremonies. It was a huge deal for me because I wasn't confident in my intelligence, and I always believed other people thought I was stupid. Standing up onstage during all the ceremonies felt like concrete evidence that maybe I wasn't so dumb after all.

My school had a very strict dress code, so I was careful about picking out the dress I had to wear during the ceremonies. (I had already been suspended earlier that year because my bra strap was showing.) I made sure that I didn't buy anything that was spaghetti strapped, that showed cleavage, or that was too short. Despite my efforts, after the first ceremony I was asked to report to the teacher in charge because there was a "problem" with my dress.

I remember walking into her room so clearly. She was wearing a blue floral dress, and ironically, her thick bra straps peaked out the sides when she leaned over. Her class was full of twenty-some geometry students getting an early start on their homework. I walked right up to her desk and said quietly, "I was told there was a problem with my dress."

"Yeah." She didn't bother to whisper so the whole class looked up. "It's breaking the dress code."

"No, it's not," I protested. "It's not short, low cut, or spaghetti strapped."

"That dress is too tight for *your* body. And the dress code clearly prohibits anything that is lewd, vulgar, or obscene."

It wasn't the dress that was the problem, it was my body—more specifically, my boobs. Unless I could find a dress that hid my breasts and didn't look the slightest bit "suggestive," I wouldn't be allowed to take part in the graduation ceremonies. The ultimatum verified what I had suspected: the teacher in charge thought I shouldn't be showcased as one of the top of the class because I didn't look like someone whose intelligence deserved to be acknowledged.

Some girls don't have a problem understanding that they can be an intelligent woman and a sexual being at the same time. Others feel stuck in one role or the other. Many girls who speak up a lot in class and make good grades don't feel like they're the type of girl that guys want to date. And many girls who are confident in their appearance and their sexuality don't feel as positive about their intelligence.

The idea that a girl is either smart or sexy is probably most evident in a school setting. Think about the girls you know: are the girls who are considered "smart" the same girls who are considered "hot" or vice versa? Probably not. But smart girls aren't any less likely than anyone else to be good looking or sexy. And there is nothing about being attractive that makes a girl more likely to be dumb.

Since we don't generally associate being smart with being sexy, we don't see smart girls as sexy, and they don't see themselves that way either. Girls who are "sexy" may get so used to the message that only their appearance matters that they don't make as much of an effort in class. This stereotype can be incredibly damaging to girl's self-esteem because it affects how desirable we believe we are and how seriously we take ourselves.

If you are a "smart girl": Being smart doesn't mean that you don't have a sexual side that you can focus on if you want to. If you can convince yourself that you're sexy, other people will start to see you that way as well. Being smart isn't a turn-off, and, although a few guys may be intimidated, the good ones will be excited to talk to someone who has interesting and intelligent things to say. Especially as you get older, you'll find that guys value intelligence in a partner and are very turned on by intellectual women. Being smart doesn't isolate you from the sexual world; in fact, it gives you a leg up.

If you are a "sexy girl": If you're a girl who is often complimented on your looks, you may not always be as praised for your intellectual abilities. That does not, however, mean that you are stupid. How another person judges your intelligence is a reflection on them, not an accurate measure of your abilities. Being attractive doesn't have to be all you are, or mean that your thoughts and opinions don't need to be heard. The better you are able to see yourself as an intelligent being, the more seriously other people will take you.

WOMEN DON'T GET HORNY OR ENJOY SEX AS MUCH AS MEN DO

Stereotypically, women aren't supposed to want sex. We're like the sexual benchwarmers; we're supposed to get all dressed up to play (makeup, cleavage, tight pants), but then we can't go out on the field (or we're "slutty" if we do). And since we're not *supposed* to want sex, many people believe that women *actually* don't want it. Some people think that women don't get horny or that, if they do, they don't get nearly as horny as men. Sure it's true that women may be more hesitant than men to engage in sex, but that's not because we desire it less.

Guys are raised to be in touch with their sexual side. They are bombarded with pictures of half-naked women in poses that imply, "Hey, baby, wanna screw?" Name a typical "guy thing," like sports games or beer commercials, and there are usually hot, half-naked girls connected with it. Furthermore, the American idea of a "man" is a guy who wants to get it on as much as possible.

Imagine if the world tried to make us permanently horny in the same way it does to guys. What if our girly magazines were filled with pictures of ridiculously hot, naked men? What if shows like *Oprah* had hot male cheerleaders who shook their asses every time she made a good point? And what if "being a lady" meant behaving like a porn star? It seems ridiculous, but that's essentially the world that guys grow up in. Guys don't want sex more than girls, or get hornier than we do; it's just that they've been taught it's OK to express their sexual desires, whereas we're supposed to suppress ours.

Girls may be more hesitant to engage in sex acts, but it's not because we desire sex less than guys do. We just have more to lose. When a guy has sex, he's a "pimp"—he's not going to get himself pregnant, and his chance of catching an STD is half that of a girl's. And even if he's having sex for the first time, he's likely to have an orgasm.

When a girl has sex, she has to worry about people frowning upon her "dirty" decision. She has to deal with the anxiety of a possible pregnancy and the increased chance of catching an STD. And even after risking all that, there's a good chance that she won't even get off. So if women are slower to want to jump in the sack, it's not because our sex drive isn't as strong—it's because sex is riskier for girls than it is for guys.

The problem with thinking that women don't get horny or don't want sex is that it makes sex something that we do for guys and not for ourselves. It sets us up to feel used and dirty when having sex because we're told that we don't really want to be doing it. And it completely undermines our sexual satisfaction because if women don't want sex, what does it matter if we enjoy it? We have to acknowledge our sexual desires and needs, because it's not fair to go into sexual encounters thinking a guy's experience is more important than our own.

SCREW THE STEREOTYPES—SEX SHOULD BE EMPOWERING

You can't control that our society has negative stereotypes about women and sexuality, or that you will be exposed to them. You can, however, refuse to let these stereotypes dictate your actions and your thoughts. You can stop yourself the next time you're tempted to call a girl a slut because she slept with someone. If some guy calls you an airhead, you can say, "You're just jealous that I'm sexier than you are." And the next time you overhear a boy being grossed out by menstruation, you can ask him why he's so scared of a little bit of blood.

Stereotypes about women's sexuality have been deeply ingrained in our society and may be impossible to completely change. But we can change the way we see and judge ourselves and, equally as important, the way we see and judge each other.

Chapter 12
Body Image
Flaws and All

I will admit, I have spent an embarrassing amount of time in front of the mirror poking, tucking, and pinching my body. I have stood there naked for hours wondering why my thighs have to be so big and what I could possibly do to make them smaller. I have stretched out the skin on my stomach until it is completely flat and thought about how good I would feel if my stomach were just a little bit tighter. And I have stared so long at my profile that I've convinced myself that my nose is taking over my face.

And then I'll have days when I'll decide that big thighs are sexy and that having a big nose makes my face more interesting. I'll eat a couple cookies and not feel the least bit guilty. (Who really cares about a flat stomach anyway?) And I'll look at myself in the mirror and not think twice about my honker. Then, not a week later, I'll be back in the gym for an hour and a half trying to slim down my thighs and back at the mirror trying to tuck my nose into my nostrils.

Being happy with your body and your appearance can be like a tug-of-war. Some days you may feel great about what you look like; some days you may decide you don't care; and other days you may just be flat-out disgusted. This chapter is about why we dislike what we look like, how to like what we look like, and how to stay healthy.

WHY WE DON'T LIKE HOW WE LOOK

It's hard to be completely satisfied with your appearance when you're a girl. Many of the women around us seem to obsess over what they look like; advertisements for products to make us look better are everywhere, and what is "beautiful" is defined very narrowly and without much wiggle room. When we see an advertisement, look through a magazine, or watch television, we're shown images of "ideal beauty." And when we're shown what features are "ideally beautiful," we aren't exactly given many options. When was the last time you saw a model with a big nose; small, beady eyes; or love handles? In the media, "beautiful" women, for the most part, look the same (or at least have the same "perfect" features).

What the media portrays as "beautiful" is not what most girls actually look like. As a result, many girls feel unattractive, even if they are very pretty. But as insecure as media portrayals of beauty can make you feel, they are virtually inescapable. It's not realistic, or even necessarily desirable, to completely avoid magazines, movies, or television. But what you can do is be aware of how the media's idea of "beauty" makes you feel about your appearance. If you are aware of how different forms of media tap into your insecurities, you'll be better equipped to stay positive regardless of what you see on TV.

BEING HAPPIER WITH HOW YOU LOOK

Being happy with how you look can take time—and it's often an uphill battle. The best way to stay positive is to keep things in perspective. (Whatever bothers you about your appearance probably isn't as catastrophic as it may sometimes feel.) The following are some things that I like to think about when trying to feel more confident about how I look.

* Everyone has "flaws." Nearly every woman in the world (supermodels and actresses included) has something she doesn't like about her body. No matter how perfect another girl may look to us, she is probably unsatisfied with some aspect of her appearance. And this tells us two things. First, there is no such thing

as "perfect" because everyone's idea of perfection is different. And second, your "flaws" are the things that *you* don't like about your appearance, not the things that are objectively "wrong" with how you look.

When girls look at their bodies, they often take a part of it and decide if it's a good or bad attribute. You may look at your butt and think, "I hate how big my butt is," while some guy who looks at your butt is thinking, "Hell, yeah, baby, back that ass up." The things that many of us find wrong with our bodies are often things that other people may not notice, or may even find attractive.

✳ The pictures you see in magazines are images—not reality. The thing to remember about celebrities is that even they don't look like celebrities. When beautiful actresses and models wake up in the morning, they don't naturally look amazing. When they aren't wearing makeup, don't have their hair professionally done, and aren't decked out in designer clothing, they look just like normal people. When you look at a girl in a magazine (be it a celebrity cover shot or a photo of a model), you're looking at the best picture out of thousands. You're also looking at an image that has probably been airbrushed to make her skin brighter, her waist smaller, her legs longer, and her boobs bigger. If you found the best picture ever taken of yourself, and then digitally altered it to make yourself look even better, you'd look pretty damn amazing, too.

✳ Concentrate on what you like about your looks, not what you don't. There may be things about your appearance that you don't like. But what is the point of dwelling on them? All that will do is make you feel bad. Instead, you should focus on the parts of your body that you do like. Wear clothes or makeup that show those parts off. Think about how lucky you are to have your "good parts," instead of focusing on what you consider your "less-good parts."

✳ Remember that feeling unattractive is a feeling. When you're feeling unattractive, it's important to remember that it is just an emotion. *Feeling* unattractive doesn't mean that you look bad—it means you feel bad. Sometimes "feeling ugly" is a sign that something else is bothering you, and your negative feelings are surfacing through feeling unattractive. In reality, what you're upset about may have nothing to do with your appearance at all.

✳ It's more important to be a cool person than just to be good looking. When it comes down to it, wanting to be attractive generally boils down to wanting people to like you. In the long run, having a great personality and a kind-hearted nature is going to win over more people than what you look like. Besides, your personality lasts a lifetime; your looks don't.

✳ Be confident. When it comes to initial attraction, you may not believe that it's what's on the inside that counts. But the way that a girl feels about herself on the inside often makes her attractive on the outside. Girls who are confident and who *feel* attractive carry themselves better, act "sexier," and ultimately attract more people than girls who don't have as positive a self-image. When I think about my friends who are the most well-liked (by guys and girls), they're the ones who are confident, not necessarily the best looking. If you're having trouble feeling confident, you can always fake it to other people. Pretty soon, how you feel will catch up with how you act.

REACHING PEACE WITH YOUR BODY

Honestly, I really don't know any girl who truly loves every part of her body 100 percent of the time. But I do know many girls who truly love themselves, flaws and all. Many women aren't satisfied with the appearance of their bodies until maybe they're ninety and don't care what their body looks like anymore, as long as it's still working properly. (And truth be told, even then, they may not be happy.) If you're like most women, there will be parts of your body you love, parts of your body you like, and parts of your body you can't stand.

Coming to peace with your body is realizing that it's OK if there are things about your appearance that you don't find perfect. You have to ask yourself, "So what?" Is the fact that you're "big boned," that you'll "always have love handles," or that you have "funny-looking ears" really going to mean anything in the grand scheme of your life? Probably not. Your physical "flaws" will not stop you from falling in love, being successful, or accomplishing something noteworthy. Nothing that you find "wrong" about how you look is going to impact anything truly important in your life.

It's a mistake to let something you don't love about your appearance affect the way you feel about yourself. Your personality, your talents, your ambition, and your kindness are the things that actually matter. And those are the traits you should really be critiquing about yourself and focusing on improving.

WEIGHT ISSUES

I distinctly remember going to see *American Pie 2* with my boyfriend; we were cuddled up, eating popcorn, and then he said something brilliant, along the lines of "That girl's got a killer body, huh?" I remember literally spitting the popcorn out of my mouth and shoving the bag over to his side.

"I'll show him," I thought. "He thinks she looks good—wait until I lose ten pounds. What will he think then?"

When we focus on our looks, much of our attention goes to our weight. This is probably because our weight is something about our appearance that we have control over. Maybe we can't change the size of our forehead, the fullness of our lips, or the shape of our eyes, but if we want to be skinnier, we can do it. Many girls have the misconception that losing weight will help them live a more fulfilling life—that it will make them happier, make them more confident, or somehow give them a leg up. They believe that getting thinner could keep a boyfriend from checking out other girls, or make a guy who's not interested suddenly change his tune.

Our culture puts tremendous pressure on women to be thin, and it can be difficult to ignore the cues that suggest "you should be thinner." But being thinner does not equal being more attractive. And losing weight will not solve any of your problems. If you truly need to lose weight (because a doctor has suggested this may be a good idea for your health), it's one thing, but if you're at a normal, healthy weight, dieting is not something that you need to be thinking about. Girls who diet unnecessarily and exercise extreme amounts can damage and weaken their bodies. And it's always more important for your body to be healthy than it is for your body to be thin.

WEIGHT LOSS GONE TOO FAR

Note: Eating disorders are a common and complex problem for young women. This chapter only begins to scrape the surface. For more detailed information about eating disorders, see the sources at the end of this chapter.

Between five million and ten million people in the United States are currently suffering from an eating disorder. The majority of these people are women, and many of them developed their disorder as a teenager. Eating disorders can cause permanent organ damage and, in some cases, death.

There are two types of eating disorders that commonly affect teenage girls: anorexia and bulimia. Girls who have anorexia obsess over eating a very small amount of food because they are intensely afraid of becoming fat. Although they may lose weight very rapidly and be very skinny, when they look in the mirror they may see someone who is much larger.

Girls who suffer from anorexia refuse to maintain a normal body weight, and, as a result, they stop getting their periods and greatly damage their bodies. Some signs of anorexia include an extreme and continual fear of gaining weight, not eating or eating only very little, having strict food rituals (like chewing a certain number of times or always having to eat in a certain order), developing an excessive fuzzy coat of hair all over their face and body, losing excessive amounts of weight, losing hair, and constantly feeling cold.

Girls who are bulimic will eat but will then feel that they need to get rid of the food (called "purging") by either throwing it up, taking laxatives, overexercising, or starving themselves afterward. Most bulimics are very preoccupied with the appearance of their body, and judge themselves based upon how their bodies look.

When bulimics eat they may "binge" instead of eating a normal meal. During a binge, a person eats an abnormally large amount of food within a small amount of time and feels that she cannot stop or control her eating. After binging, someone with bulimia often feels guilty, shameful, or fearful of how the food will affect her body and "purges" to get rid of it.

Although many anorexic girls become very thin, bulimics often maintain an average weight because purging doesn't actually get rid of the majority of calories from a binge. But like anorexics, bulimics seriously damage many organs by the stress that throwing up or taking laxatives has upon their bodies. Some signs of bulimia include being preoccupied with food, eating a large amount of food (often in secret), throwing up after eating, taking laxatives, constantly feeling the need to exercise for long periods of time, swollen glands, and broken blood vessels in the eyes from throwing up.

Because early detection and treatment greatly minimizes the damage that an eating disorder will have on one's body, it's important to be able to recognize the warning signs of an eating disorder. The following are signs that someone's diet, desire to lose weight, or control over her food intake has gone too far.

✳ *Constantly thinking about food, weight, and calories.* If someone is always thinking about how many calories she has eaten, is constantly planning out her meals, or has become so preoccupied with eating or exercising that it interferes with her daily life and relationships with friends and family, she may have an eating disorder.

* *Losing a lot of weight very quickly because of a strict diet.* If someone eats a very small amount of food each day and is losing more than one to two pounds a week, she may have an eating disorder.

* *Signs that your body "just isn't functioning right."* Missing three periods in a row, having very little energy, and feeling cold all the time are signs that a girl's body is not getting enough nutrients to function normally.

* *Binging and purging.* Someone who feels out of control when she eats, and then feels that she *needs* to exercise, throw up, or take laxatives because of what she has eaten, may be bulimic.

If, after reading this section, you feel that some of the behaviors describe your eating or exercising habits, or how you feel about body weight, you should talk about your concerns with a doctor. If an eating disorder is left untreated, it can affect your health in the following ways:

* Inability to focus, concentrate or control your mood.

* Dangerously low pulse, dizziness, shortness of breath, chest pain, or sudden heart attacks.

* Stunted growth or frail bones that break easily.

* Loss of teeth, a constant sore throat, gum disease, or a bleeding esophagus from throwing up.

* Constant stomachaches, constipation, or other digestive problems.

* Permanent damage to the heart, stomach, liver, and kidneys.

* Permanent damage to the reproductive organs and the inability to have children.

No one will tell you that giving up an eating disorder is easy. Many people who are recovering from eating disorders say that, although telling someone about it was terrifying, they knew they had to get better. If you come forward about your eating disorder to someone you trust and feel comfortable with (a friend, family member, or doctor), that person will be able to provide support and get help for you. If you want to speak with a counselor anonymously before you tell anyone, or if you have any questions about eating disorders, you can call the National Eating Disorders Association at 1-800-931-2237. Overcoming an eating disorder can be a long and difficult process. But people recover all the time, are able to live happy lives, and develop a more comfortable relationship with food and eating.

BEING HEALTHY

If you want your body to be in the best shape possible, you should eat well and get regular exercise. Eating well does not mean going on a super-restrictive diet or completely cutting out carbs or fat. It means eating a balanced diet of plenty of fresh fruits and vegetables, whole grains (like whole wheat bread or oatmeal), lean meats (or lots of tofu and beans if you're a vegetarian), low-fat dairy (milk, cheese, and yogurt), and healthy fats (avocados, nuts, and olive and canola oils).

If you are going to diet (and you should speak with your doctor first to make sure that you should truly be losing weight), it's important to go about it in a healthy way. Crash diets, which promise to make you lose lots of weight in a short amount of time, don't work. Even if you do lose weight quickly, most of the weight you're losing is water, not fat. Many of the diets that claim to make you slim down quickly just dehydrate you, so that you weigh less and feel smaller. But the amount of actual fat you lose on those diets is very low. The problem with crash diets is that starving yourself will lower your metabolism and, in the long run, actually cause you to gain weight. Not only are crash diets unhealthy, but also they *do not* work.

The only diets that are successful and healthy are those that are moderate. You shouldn't be losing more than two pounds per week (or you are likely lowering your metabolism). It is never healthy to completely cut out a food group (although at the moment many of the "hot" diets will try to get you to ditch carbs), or seriously restrict the amount of food you eat. Whatever you are eating, you should never eat less than twelve hundred calories a day, and if you are exercising a great deal, you should be eating more. If you are intent about losing weight, then discuss it with your doctor.

When thinking about food, dieting, and your body, it's always good to keep two things in mind. First of all, food is not the enemy; you have to eat to live. Second of all, the purpose of your body is not to look "perfect" or be thin. The purpose of your body is to keep you alive. It is your health, and not your weight, that is the most important.

FURTHER INFORMATION

* About Face (body image): http://www.about-face.org

* Alliance for Eating Disorders Awareness (information about eating disorders): http://www.eatingdisorderinfo.org

* National Eating Disorders Association (information about eating disorders): http://www.nationaleatingdisorders.org

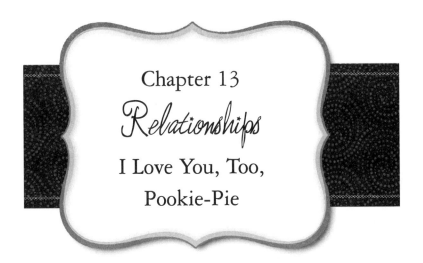

Chapter 13

Relationships

I Love You, Too, Pookie-Pie

*M*y first serious relationship played out like a trashy talk show. I was fifteen, a sophomore in high school, and I didn't know what it was like to have a guy really care about me. When my boyfriend said he loved me, I was sold. I couldn't believe that I was saying "I love you" to someone other than my parents—it was a dream come true.

But as "in love" as we were, it didn't take very long for us to stop getting along completely. We became our own traveling circus. We'd go to parties together and make *huge* scenes. It would start over something completely insignificant, then escalate into us both screaming, sobbing, and needing emotional support from everyone else there. For months we would break up every Saturday night, and every Sunday afternoon we'd get back together.

It was obvious that our relationship wasn't healthy, but we were "in love," and that was the trump card. Sure, we had nonsensical blowouts about everything from tight shirts to trailer parks, but the fact that we loved each other seemed bigger than all of it. As bad as things were, we were determined to stay together. And we did for a little over a year, but, after a dozen or so daylong breakups, we finally ended it for good.

My first relationship was probably a bit more dysfunctional than most, but where the details are different, the general experience is the same. Being "in love" for the first time can give you the judgment of the village drunk. Relationships can be totally blinding and can cause you to make some really bad decisions. This chapter is about getting into relationships, keeping them healthy, and how to keep going when they end.

GUYS TO BE WARY OF

When you first start dating a guy, there isn't any way to know for sure how the relationship is going to work out or how well the guy is going to treat you. Although it's never good to be overly judgmental, there are certain types of guys that you should probably avoid. This is not to say you definitely shouldn't date them, only that you should take an extra minute to think about it. If you find yourself getting involved with one of the following types of guys, you may want to reconsider.

Mr. Not-Quite-Right. When girls are choosing a guy to date, it's not uncommon for them to pick a guy they want to change. Maybe he's a bad boy who's failing out of school, he has the emotional capacity of a robot, or he tells more lies than Pinocchio. But, no matter what his flaw, a girl will date him, thinking that she'll fix whatever is wrong with him.

Some girls date "fixer-uppers" because they find the idea of helping someone overcome their problems romantic. It may feel like living a made-for-TV movie: the drug addict falls in love with a girl and then turns his life around. When you could be that important in someone else's life, why waste your time in a boring relationship with a guy who doesn't have any problems?

Other girls date guys with obvious problems because it makes them feel more secure in the relationship. If you know there's something undesirable about the guy you're dating, then maybe you won't be afraid of him abandoning you. After all, when it comes down to it, you know you're too good for him.

But guys should not be approached like projects. Relationships are hard enough in the first place, without there being something fundamentally "wrong" with the guy you're dating from the beginning. Sure, a guy can change, but for it to be a lasting change, he has to do it for himself, not for someone else. Although it may be scarier to get involved with a guy who has a lot going for him, you deserve to be with a good guy. The point of relationships is not to help fix someone—if you want to help people, volunteer at your local homeless shelter. But don't date a loser. Not every guy you date has to be Mr. Right, but don't date someone who you know from the beginning is Mr. Wrong.

Mr. Irresistible. Everyone knows him. He's messed around with numerous girls, broken hearts, and has jumped from crush to crush like a flea jumps from dog to dog. And yet, girls continue to fall for him. By "Mr. Irresistible," I don't just mean a guy who's popular (popular guys aren't necessarily jerks)—I mean a guy who is known for pursuing girls until he gets what he wants and then moves on.

Maybe you can't resist being attracted to a guy like this, but you can resist getting involved with him. These types of guys are either self-centered jerks or completely insecure. A secure guy doesn't have to make every girl want him in order to remind himself that he is desirable. And a guy who just wants to hook up with as many girls as possible is either trying to prove himself to other guys or doesn't know what he really wants.

Some girls have a personal "Mr. Irresistible"—a guy they keep going back to even though they know it will make them feel like crap in the long run. Maybe it's a guy they really like who has made it clear that he doesn't want anything serious. Or maybe it's an ex-boyfriend that they can't move past. Whether he's a fling, an ex, or just a total player, it's a bad idea to hook up with a guy knowing (or strongly suspecting) that it will leave you feeling unfulfilled and upset.

Although some guys can make you feel weak or even powerless, *you* are in control of what you do. You can curse and call him an asshole as much as you want, but if you knew the type of guy you were getting involved with, you're responsible for your own decisions. As difficult as it can be to resist a charming guy, refusing to be involved with a guy that makes you feel bad is completely empowering. Even doing it once can give you the confidence to avoid emotionally damaging relationships for good.

The much-older man. There's a lot that seems to be appealing about an older guy: he's more mature, he probably knows more about girls and relationships, and he automatically seems cooler just because he's older. But the problem with dating older guys (especially when they're much older) is that the age difference often sets up an unequal balance of power. Because the guy is likely more experienced, he may seem to have more authority in the relationship than his younger girlfriend. This can be especially problematic when it comes to sex. Many girls feel that they can't turn down sex with an older guy because the guy "just wouldn't put up with it." So if you're a virgin who wants to stay a virgin (or a non-virgin who just isn't interested in sleeping with anyone at the moment), dating an older guy may create a problem.

If you find yourself attracted to an older guy, date him only if you are confident that you can stand up for what you want in the relationship (whether that means how much time the two of you spend together, how he treats you, or how sexual you want things to get). Remember that it's always OK to say no to sex, and saying no to an older guy is no exception. You may assume that he has had lots of sexual experience and considers sex a given in a relationship. But that's probably not true. Guys of any age get turned down for sex all the time—even guys in college don't necessarily get laid that much. As intimidating as an older guy may be on the surface, he probably isn't as experienced or mature as you may assume.

"Love conquers all" sometimes. A girl can have a very equal and loving relationship with someone a few years older. But often, guys go after younger girls because they want to be in complete control of a relationship—meaning that they can treat the girl like crap and get away with it, or that they can talk the girl into sex. When a guy dates a younger girl it should be because she *happens* to be younger, not because he wants someone he can control. Although not all older guys are bad news, be wary of the potential power imbalance. And if you are going to date one, make sure you're comfortable enough to define the relationship on your own terms.

HEALTHY RELATIONSHIPS

When you start dating a guy, dishonesty and games are two of the quickest ways to damage what would otherwise be a healthy relationship. It may seem like a good idea to flirt with other guys while your boyfriend is around just to show him that other people want you. Or you may want to act like you're not that into him so that you feel that you're more in control of the relationship. But acting uninterested will not make a guy like you more than he already does; if anything it will make him too insecure to show his feelings for you.

Guys are confused enough about girls without us acting the opposite of how we actually feel. The best way to have a relationship is to be honest with the guy you're with. Don't do anything to him that you wouldn't want him to do to you. If you feel insecure about how he feels, talk with him about it instead of flirting with someone right in front of him. Tell him, "I feel like you've been acting a little weird. Is everything OK?" The more mature and respectful you are of him, the more comfortable he will feel, and the better your communication will be with each other.

It doesn't matter what kind of sexual chemistry you have with a guy; if you can't talk about the relationship and how you're feeling, it's not going to work out. It can be scary to be honest with someone about your feelings because it may make you feel vulnerable. But if you want there to be emotional intimacy in a relationship, you have to be willing to open up. You can only expect a guy to be as intimate with you as you are with him.

STAYING TRUE TO YOUR FRIENDS AND YOURSELF WHILE IN SERIOUS RELATIONSHIPS

If you get into a serious relationship, your boyfriend will become a big part of your life. But no matter how much you may care about a guy, it's important not to get lost in your relationship with him. In order to not get lost, you must remain true to yourself and your own needs.

Although it's natural to be influenced by someone you're close to, you shouldn't change your values or beliefs just because they don't match up with your boyfriend's. No matter how into a guy you are, don't give up a meaningful hobby so that you can spend more time with him. Set your own goals and priorities, even if that means pursuing a dream that may not be in the best interest of the relationship. And most important, always maintain a life outside of the one you have with your boyfriend.

Part of remaining true to yourself when you are in a relationship is being true to your friends. Many girls become distant from their girlfriends when they get a serious boyfriend. It's extremely important, and very possible, to remain close with your friends while in a relationship. After all, they're the ones you can talk to after a fight; they're the ones who will help you cope if the relationship ends; and they're the ones who are more likely to be around in five years. The following are some tips on keeping your friendships strong while you have a boyfriend.

Don't get too caught up with his friends. When you start seriously dating a guy, you're obviously going to want to get to know his friends. If you become part of his social group, you'll probably get to see him more, and you'll have a bunch of new people to hang out with. If his friends become your friends, you'll know that when problems in the relationship come up, they'll encourage him to work it out, as opposed to saying, "Dump her."

As much fun as you may have hanging out with his friends and winning them over, always remember that, when it comes down to it, they are *his* friends. This means that they're looking out for *his* best interests. And if the two of you break up, guess who they're going to sympathize with?

Don't be the annoying "this one time my boyfriend . . ." girl. Your friends want to know what's going on in your life, and they obviously care about any huge developments in your relationship. They will want to hear all about your first date, the first time you said "I love you," a giant fight the two of you got into, and how things are moving along sexually. But beyond anything really important, they don't want to hear about the cute burp he had the other day or the evening you spent with his granny patching up his favorite jeans.

Talking about your boyfriend all the time can bore your friends, but, more important, it can make them feel left out or jealous. If all you talk about is "how funny it was when Josh blah, blah, blah," then your friends may feel like he's the only thing you care about—and that their friendship isn't a meaningful part of your life anymore.

Don't fall into the boyfriend sinkhole. Although you may want to spend a lot of time with your boyfriend, you should make a conscious effort to balance your time between him and your friends. If you start spending too much time with your boyfriend, then there's probably going to be some tension when you're hanging out with your friends. Or you may feel left out because they've been spending so much time together without you. If your relationship with your friends feels weird, then it's tempting to spend even more time with your boyfriend, which makes things with your friends even worse. And that creates a downward spiral where you're with your boyfriend and his friends all of the time.

To prevent this from happening, always make and keep plans with your friends. If things feel strange when you're with them, talk about it. If they're upset with you, chances are it's because they miss you and feel like you're abandoning them. It's not that they "just don't like you anymore."

"Don't be this girl"

Let your friends know they're important to you. Communication is important in every relationship, not just romantic ones. Many girls get upset when a close friend becomes seriously involved with a guy because they're afraid it means that she won't need them anymore. It's important to let your friends know that they still play an important part in your life. Remember the things that you like to do best with your friends, and consistently make an effort to do those things with the girls you care about. They will notice and appreciate that you're still making an effort to maintain their friendships. Insecurity can bring out the worst in

anyone, and the more confident your friends are that they're still important to you, the less tension there will be when you hang out with them.

If you are on the other end of things (your friend has a boyfriend and
you feel like she's never around anymore), don't hesitate to bring it up.
Before you write her off as a crappy friend, let her know that you wish
you saw her more and that you miss her. The more honest you are with
your friends, the better you will be able to retain your friendships.

AVOIDING UNHEALTHY RELATIONSHIPS

When my friends and I would describe our "perfect man," none of us
ever thought to add "someone who isn't abusive" to our list of criteria.
We just took it as a given. We had all seen what abusive guys were like
in movies, and obviously none of us were going to get involved with a
pot-bellied redneck who was a jerk all the time. We assumed that
staying out of abusive relationships wasn't rocket science; if a guy hits
you, he's abusive, and you dump him. But as a few of my friends found
out, abuse is not that straightforward.

Sometimes abuse is hard to recognize—because right after it happens,
the guy may sob about how sorry he is, how much he loves you, and how
he'd never hurt you. And when an abusive guy isn't being abusive, he can
be a total sweetheart who seems like he would make a great boyfriend.

Any girl is at risk for getting into an abusive relationship because
there's no way to spot an abusive guy before you get to know him. Abusive
guys can be really charismatic people who have lots of friends and are really
popular. They can be smart, talented, and athletic guys who seem like a
great catch. Abusive guys aren't just greasy dudes scratching their fat bel-
lies and yelling, "Woman, git me my dinner!" If they were disgusting jerks
all the time, then way fewer women would get involved with them.

The most misleading thing about abusive relationships is that some
of the warning signs that a guy will become abusive can easily be mistaken
as romantic or protective gestures. If you notice any of the following elements at the beginning of a relationship, proceed with caution.

He gets really into you really quickly. If a new guy says he really cares
about you, it's flattering. But if a guy dramatically confesses his endless

love when you hardly know him, it's a little strange. If early on in a relationship a guy goes on about you being "the one," he's pressuring you to jump into something really serious.

When a guy is that into you, it may be hard to question him. It's obviously more tempting to think, "This guy must really be in love with me," than, "This guy has a screw loose." But be honest with yourself: if a guy's feelings for you seem a little extreme, be flattered, but also be cautious.

He gets super jealous if you so much as talk to another guy. It feels good when your boyfriend gets a little jealous when you're around other guys. A little jealousy is normal and shows you that a guy cares enough to feel protective. But a guy who gets really upset over who you spend time with or what you wear is overbearing. Your boyfriend isn't going to want you to flirt with other guys, but he shouldn't make you feel guilty for talking to a guy who is a friend of yours or for being friendly to a male acquaintance. If a new guy won't let you wear a certain outfit, or he makes you feel guilty about talking to an old guy friend, it's not cute; it's controlling.

He wants you to spend all your time with him. You might initially be flattered by a guy who always wants to be around you. But if he *needs* to be with you every second, that's not a good sign. In a healthy relationship, both you and your boyfriend should have lives (friends and interests) aside from each other. If a guy wants to spend all his time with you, that means that in return he's expecting you to spend all your time with him. When you think about it that way, his desire to be around you seems more demanding than endearing.

Although many girls are brought up with the "Romeo fantasy"—a lover who will kill himself if he can't be with them—that kind of dependency is unhealthy; Romeo isn't so much a romantic as he is a codependent nut-job. If a guy is too affectionate (to the point where it's weird) and overly demanding of your time and attention, be careful. You may want to ask yourself, "Is this guy sweet, or are his feelings extreme, illogical, and kinda creepy?"

An abusive guy will try to consume a girl's life and isolate her from friends and family. That way, when he starts abusing her, it's not as easy for her to get out of the relationship because she has cut off attachments from loved ones. If you are ever in a relationship with a guy who seems obsessed with you, be sure that he is just trying to be sweet, not trying to pull you away from important people in your life.

RECOGNIZING ABUSE

Abuse in relationships isn't always as clear-cut as a guy who beats his girlfriend. Relationships can be abusive both physically and emotionally, and abusive behaviors aren't always obvious. The following are ways in which a guy may be abusive.

* He is overly jealous, possessive, and demanding. He needs to know where his girlfriend is at all times, what she is doing, and whom she's with. He expects his girlfriend to be with him upon his request and gets angry or upset when she hangs out with other people. He tries to isolate her from her friends and family.

* He is controlling. He tries to control what his girlfriend wears, the classes she takes, the type of job she gets, or what she does as a hobby. He tries to tell her whom she can and can't hang out with.

* He makes threats. He tells his girlfriend that if she breaks up with him he will hurt her, himself, or someone else. He tells his girlfriend he will spread lies about her or tell her friends and family something private if he does not get his way.

* He tries to embarrass, humiliate, and upset his girlfriend. He puts his girlfriend down, calls her names, and insults her. He may even do this in public to try to humiliate her. He may also try to play it all off as a joke.

* He pressures his girlfriend to do sexual acts she is not comfortable with. He tries to intimidate or guilt his girlfriend into engaging in sex acts. He may refuse to wear a condom, or make his girlfriend feel bad if she asks him to wear one.

❋ He gets violent. He has hit, or threatened to hit his girlfriend. He grabs her, pushes her, shakes her, kicks her, or strangles her. He breaks things in front of her, blocks doors, or throws things near her so that she becomes frightened.

❋ He blames his girlfriend for "making" him act a certain way. Instead of taking responsibility when he is abusive, he blames his girlfriend for his actions. He tries to make her feel as though she "deserved it" and that it is her fault.

GETTING OUT

Many girls who end up in abusive relationships have trouble getting out of them. Abusive men are often excellent negotiators and excel at "winning a girl back." An abusive guy may beg, cry, and swear that he will never do it again. He may make hugely romantic gestures and be just as sweet and wonderful as he was at the beginning of the relationship.

But abuse is a cycle. During the good times it may seem like he could never hurt a fly; but if he has been abusive before, he is likely to be abusive again.

Some girls put up with continued abuse because they're afraid that their boyfriend is the best—or only—guy they can get. An abusive guy may try to convince his girlfriend that he loves her more than anyone else ever could. He may even try to convince her that his behavior is a result of "how much he cares." But normal people don't intentionally harm the people they love; the majority of guys are capable of falling madly in love without being overly controlling or hurtful.

If you suspect that you're in a relationship with a guy who is abusive, talk with someone about it, and get help. For assistance with recognizing abusive situations, and advice on how to get out of them safely, call the National Domestic Violence Hotline at 1-800-799-7233. Despite what an abusive guy may tell you, there *are* other guys out there who will care about you in the same way that he does. The difference is that they will be able to show it without hurting you.

DEALING WITH BREAKUPS

My first breakup was one of the hardest experiences of my life. Ending it with my boyfriend meant giving up not only my first love but also the whole new group of friends that I had made in the past year, and that felt lonely. Being his girlfriend had become so much a part of my identity that I couldn't imagine my life without him in it. I was terrified that he was as good as it got and that I would never be in love again.

Mourning the loss of a boyfriend is often more about mourning the loss of love than the actual guy. When you're dealing with a breakup, it's important to separate your feelings about having *someone*, from your feelings about that *particular* someone. Most of what upset me about my first breakup was losing my boyfriend's friends and losing his place in my life, not actually losing *him*. It's possible that the things you liked so much about your boyfriend were having someone to cuddle with, having someone you feel close to, and having someone to comfort you when you were upset. Those things have nothing to do with who a guy actually is, or his personality; they are elements of any serious relationship.

When a relationship ends, it's normal to catastrophize that there "isn't anyone else," that no guy will ever love you again, or that you have just broken up with "The One." But that's never true. I know people who have gotten divorced in their sixties and still found other loves (and at that point it has to be slim pickings). The thing to remember is that there are plenty of other guys out there; you just may not have met them yet.

Truth be told, I don't know any girl who looks back on her first few relationships and thinks, "Those guys were gems; I never should have let them slip away." Most girls will tell you their boyfriends have gotten increasingly better as they go along. The more experience you have, the better you are able to figure out what kinds of guys are compatible with you. As hard as it is to break up with someone you love, something better will come along.

Breakups can be excruciating, but the pain does go away. Although it may be hard to imagine a time when you'll feel whole again, you will heal eventually. It's just like jamming your finger—the first few minutes are agonizing, but after that it's just a little bit sore. One day, a few months down the road, you'll realize that you've gotten over the breakup and that you're OK. It may take a while, but eventually, you'll be every bit as happy as you were before your boyfriend.

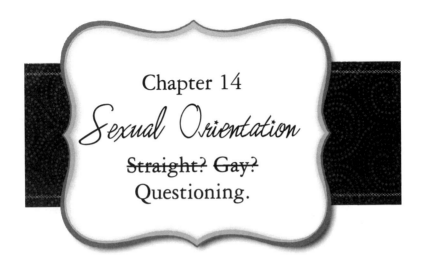

Chapter 14
Sexual Orientation
~~Straight? Gay?~~
Questioning.

*I*t all started with the book *Rubyfruit Jungle* by Rita Mae Brown. The main character was a lesbian, and after reading it, my friends and I decided that homosexuality was awesome. We all wanted to do it, as though it was a class that we could have signed up for. We went to a conservative Southern high school and would yell out "I'm a lesbian" at lunch because it was funny to watch people freak out. But as openly as we joked about being lesbians, we never actually talked about whether we had ever had sexual feelings for a girl; we just avoided the issue.

Even at 3:00 AM during sleepovers, when all the good stuff came out, it was always: "If you had to have sex with someone in our English class, who would it be?" or "Do you think I could seduce our hot student teacher?" We never asked, "Is there a girl you secretly want to kiss?" or, "Have you ever wondered if you're not completely straight?"

Then, after graduating, all the things that we "just didn't talk about" came bursting out.

"I always felt like you hated me for dating Jim."

"Well, I'm not a lesbian, but I was kinda sexually attracted to you sophomore year."

As it turned out, we all had our girl fantasies, girl crushes, and girl dreams, and most of us had wondered if we were really as straight as we thought. We had never talked about it because we each assumed that we were the only ones who had had gay thoughts.

At some point, most people will have an experience (or multiple experiences) that makes them question which sex they are *really* attracted to. Maybe you start to realize that guys just don't really do it for you. Or perhaps you're having sexual dreams about girls or get turned on when you see them naked. This chapter is about figuring out if you're attracted to girls and what to do if you think you may be gay.

WHY QUESTION YOUR SEXUALITY?

The possibility of being gay can be pretty daunting. If you're a lesbian, you'll have to sort out your own feelings, come out to your friends and family, and deal with a society that is still learning to accept homosexuals. It may be tempting to ignore any nagging feelings that you might be a lesbian and to go on dating and having sexual experiences with guys. It probably seems like it's *easier* to bury your feelings and just act heterosexual like "everyone else." If it ain't broke, don't try to fix it, right?

The problem with the "bottle it up" approach is that ignoring your feelings will make you feel more stressed and more alone than if you are honest with yourself about your sexual orientation. As difficult as it may be to question your sexuality and potentially come out as a lesbian, any lesbian will tell you that it's worth it. When lesbian or bisexual girls finally come out to themselves and others, they feel relieved not to have to continue living a lie.

Some girls start to realize that they *may* be a lesbian around the time they're twelve or thirteen. But most girls don't start to deal with their feelings until a couple of years later. Understanding your sexual preference is generally a process. It's usually not as simple as waking up one morning and thinking, "I don't want to eat a bologna sandwich for lunch today, and, gee, I don't think I'm straight either." There may be many times when you waver back and forth, wondering what your sexual orientation "really" is. Although you can talk with other people in the process, ultimately it's something you will have to figure out for yourself. If you are questioning your sexuality, the following are some things you should consider.

SEXUAL PREFERENCE IS A CONTINUUM

Most people see sexual preference in terms of black and white—as though all girls belong to one of two groups: "boy crazies," who are 100 percent straight, or "butch lesbians," who are 100 percent gay. So if you have a history of being attracted to guys and you find yourself attracted to a girl, it can be very confusing: if you're straight, you may feel like you shouldn't be attracted to girls; if you're gay, you may feel like you shouldn't have had any past attraction to boys. And if you're not totally straight and you're not totally gay, then what the hell are you?

Well, you're probably a little (or a lot) bisexual, just like most everyone else in the world. Although many people's lives would be much less confusing if we were all attracted to one sex without exception, realistically, not many people are completely gay or completely straight. Sexual preference is a continuum, and your sexual orientation is probably somewhere along that continuum, not totally at one end or the other.

Because of this continuum, it's completely possible for you to be straight and have some sexual feelings toward girls. It's also possible to be a lesbian and have some sexual feelings toward guys. The label of "straight" or "gay" is based on what you prefer *most* of the time, but it won't necessarily hold true all the time.

SEXUAL ACTS IN AND OF THEMSELVES
DO NOT DETERMINE YOUR SEXUALITY

Sexual preference is more about sexual feelings than it is about sexual acts. You can hook up with guys, but that doesn't necessarily make you straight, just as hooking up with girls doesn't in and of itself make you a lesbian. Your sexual identity is defined by how you *feel*, which may not always be what you *do*.

Some girls who consider themselves to be very straight may have kissed one of their girl friends just to see what it was like, or made out with another girl for show. Others, especially when they were younger, may have gone even further. Just because you may have had a homosexual experience, it does not necessarily mean that you're a homosexual.

Similarly, if you're very attracted to girls, hooking up with guys will not make you straight. If you are questioning your sexuality, it may be tempting to prove to yourself that you "really are straight" by hooking up with as many guys as possible. But carelessly hooking up with a lot of guys can lead to serious consequences (like pregnancy or STDs), and it won't give you a clearer picture of your sexuality or "turn you straight again." If you are a lesbian, you are a lesbian. Sleeping with a bunch of guys, or getting yourself pregnant, is not going to change that.

YOU MIGHT BE A LESBIAN IF . . .

There *are* signs that you might be a lesbian or bisexual, but they may not be the signs you think. Having short hair, wearing baggy clothes, liking sports, and not being into makeup and fashion has nothing to do with whether or not you are gay. And being into "girly" things like nail polish and bubble baths doesn't necessarily mean that you're straight. Although many people believe all lesbians look like "dykes" and act "manly," there isn't an all encompassing lesbian look or way of acting. Lesbians come from all religions, nationalities, races, and social classes. The only "signs" that you are a lesbian or bisexual are indications that you are physically and emotionally attracted to other women. And those signs look like this.

Disclaimer: Because hardly anyone is completely straight or completely gay, it's possible that you may look at this list and think, "Sometimes yes, and sometimes no." Having occasional sexual thoughts about girls may not mean anything. If you find, however, that you're having many sexual thoughts about girls (and not boys), then it's probably something that you want to pay attention to.

✳ *You can't get into the prince charming fantasy.* While all your friends may be talking about guys that are hot and guys they want to date, you just can't get into it. Perhaps there is nothing about the idea of being with a guy that seems all that exciting to you. You don't have to be totally obsessed, but most straight girls occupy at least part of their minds with thoughts about guys. (Note: some girls don't start feeling sexually attracted to guys until they are older. That doesn't mean that they're lesbians—it means that they haven't started having sexual feelings.)

✳ *You wish you could date your friends.* It's one thing to want to find the same emotional compatibility in a guy that you have with your close girl friends. But if you are constantly wishing that you could find guys who were *just like* your girl friends, it's possible that you actually wish you could date your friends, not a guy who's just like them.

✳ *You just feel different, like you don't fit in.* Especially as a teenager, every girl has times when she feels like an outsider. But many lesbians say that from a young age they just knew that something about them was different from other girls. At the time they couldn't put their finger on what it was, but they always felt that there was some way that they just didn't fit in with the girls they knew.

✳ *You find yourself* looking *at other girls.* All girls look at other girls. We look at them in magazines, watch them on TV, and check them out as they're walking down the street. But there is a difference between looking at them for comparison and looking at them sexually. On the next page is a chart that distinguishes looking (just to look) from *looking* (lusting).

If you are questioning your sexual orientation, you're probably a little annoyed, confused, and scared. Here, the one thing you thought you knew for sure about sex (that you wanted to do it with boys) is getting turned upside down. As frustrating as it may be, the best thing to do is try to stay in touch with your feelings. You don't have to keep your feelings bottled up inside; you can write your thoughts down in a journal, read books about young lesbians' experiences, or talk to a counselor, your friends, or other girls going through a similar experience. It may take a while to understand how you're feeling, but if you stay honest with yourself, you'll figure it out eventually.

Looking	Lusting
"I want my butt to look like hers!"	**or** "I really want to touch her butt!"
"That girl has huge boobs!"	**or** "I want to use her boobs as a pillow."
"She has really plump lips."	**or** "I would really love to kiss her."
"Guys must love to watch her dance."	**or** "Watching her dance is really turning me on!"

The following is one girl's story about figuring out her sexuality.

DISCOVERING MY SEXUALITY: BY BETSY GOLDMAN, 21

Before this year, I had never sat down to think about, or write about, my questioning and coming-out experience. And when I started to think about it, I realized it was like this tsunami of confusion, fear, and change flooding over me. For years I had ducked under that wave, avoiding what it meant that I was dating girls. I had been avoiding what it meant to call myself gay, a lesbian, a homo. The easy part—believe it or not—was telling my friends and family. The hard part was understanding myself not only as a sexual woman but as a homosexual woman.

I started questioning my sexuality when I was thirteen or fourteen. It started out slowly—I was interested in the subculture of gay life and obsessed with the play *Rent*. Then it began to grow—I talked about gay rights with anyone who would listen, wanted to wear rainbows just to see people's reactions, and started a gay/straight alliance at my high school. Now, one might think that, since my involvement in gay "things" was building, that my coming out (to myself or others) would have been like fireworks or something. Actually, it was more like a pop and a fizzle—no sparks or anything.

One afternoon in ninth grade, I left chorus early with a bad stomachache. I used to get stomachaches often, but I knew how to calm myself down from them. I needed to write. It sounds funny, I know, but for some reason writing down what was going on in my head took the pain away from my stomach. So I headed for the nurse and borrowed a pad of paper and a pen.

I still have the piece of paper—it's like evidence to me. While sitting on the bed in the nurse's office, I wrote: "Am I still really uncomfortable with the fact that after months and months of denying it, I've finally admitted it to myself that I'm bi (maybe even with a preference to girls)?" It's there, in the middle of the page, surrounded by other sentences, so that page looks completely normal—completely harmless.

Now, at this point, you might think that I would have done something about my discovery. I had been active in gay rights that year, and I already had accepting friends (proven by a friend of mine who was coming out). It would have made sense to have come out and started my life as bi, maybe even bi with a preference for girls.

This, however, was not the case. After that day, I misplaced that piece of paper and—this is the only way I can think to put it—forgot about it for four years. I don't know why or how it happened, but even after writing it down, I didn't think I was gay. Throughout high school, I had crushes on and dated boys. (Well, I didn't date a lot of boys, but still.) My thoughts about boys, and the encounters I had with them, were on par with a typical straight teenage girl. It wasn't until four years later that I started to remember.

When I was a freshman in college, I started dating a boy. The problem was, I had become great friends with a very charismatic, very out lesbian, who had a crush on me.

At first, I thought nothing of it. However, after a few weeks, I began to feel something that was both familiar and completely foreign. I started to realize that I didn't have feelings for the guy I was dating—I had feelings for this girl. Having a crush was natural, but the fact that it was for a girl was something I was not expecting. I wrote an e-mail to a lesbian friend of mine to ask her advice, and by the time she had gotten back to me, the very out lesbian and I had kissed.

Four years after I first realized it, almost to the day, I let myself be with a girl.

In a way, it's impossible for me to put into words the feelings of questioning, realization, coming out, and (perhaps most important) becoming comfortable after coming out. It can feel like you're being swallowed whole by a wave, a lion, yourself. It can feel exciting, like a roller coaster. It can also feel like taking a deep breath in for the first time—full, light, comforting.

It has been four years since I first came out, and though I've become increasingly comfortable in my body and my head, I still think about who I am sexually. Since I came out, I have dated both girls and boys, but I do not identify myself as bisexual. I do, however, know two things: I know that I feel warmer when I think about being with a girl. When I think about dating girls, something inside of me clicks—and that's what I have to pay attention to. I also know that no matter who I end up kissing, dating, or loving, and whatever label I affix to my sexuality, the core of me will never change—I will always be me, and that is very comforting.

I'm Pretty Sure I'm a Lesbian—So Now What?

Realizing that you like girls doesn't mean your next move has to be shouting to the world that you're a lesbian. Depending on your situation, you may decide not to tell anyone. In any case, there are many support groups, organizations, and counselors that can help talk you through your feelings and help you decide whom (if anyone) you should come out to. If you realize you're a lesbian, keep this in mind.

✳ *You are not alone.* Even if you want to keep your sexuality a secret, you don't have to come to terms with it on your own. There are many other girls going through the same thing that you are, and if you want to talk with them anonymously, that's easy to do with online chat rooms. If you don't have private access to the Internet, you can call the toll-free National Gay and Lesbian Youth Hotline. (The phone numbers and Web addresses are listed at the end of this chapter.)

✳ *You are still normal.* Being sexually attracted to girls may mean that you are either bisexual or homosexual, but it doesn't mean you're a freak. Homosexuality is completely normal; people have been realizing that they are homosexual for thousands of years. There is nothing wrong, disgusting, or weird about girls liking other girls.

✳ *You are still at risk.* Even if you are going to start hooking up with girls, you still have to worry about STDs. When you are hooking up with another girl, use an oral dam during oral sex, don't share sex toys, and don't let any of your bodily fluids (menstrual or vaginal discharge/lubrication) come into contact with her vagina, mouth, or anus, and vice versa. And, if you are still going to be hooking up with guys, make sure you protect yourself from both STDs and pregnancy.

✳ *It will be OK.* As confused and scared as you may be right now, things will get easier. There's lots of support available to lesbians, and many communities are becoming increasingly tolerant and accommodating toward both young and old homosexuals. With time, you will be completely comfortable being a lesbian, and you will be proud of your lesbian identity.

Top Ten Reasons Why Being a Lesbian Is *Awesome*:
By Amanda Deibert, 23

10. Your girlfriend will always remind you to take your birth control—oh, wait, you don't have to.

9. You'll never get stubble burn from a woman—well, you'll never get stubble burn from making out with a woman.

8. Spit or swallow? No longer a dilemma.

7. Sex can go on for hours without pause for "recovery" time.

6. Hooking up with your partner in a public restroom is a lot easier.

5. Having a girlfriend is a fantastic wardrobe extender.

4. A girl won't feel awkward talking about her feelings or your relationship. As a matter of fact, you'll spend hours doing just that.

3. When you hook up with a girl, she'll know where your clit is.

2. Your girlfriend will understand that your chocolate cravings and mood swings don't mean that you've stopped loving her.

1. Sex and relationships are always better with someone you are actually attracted to and could fall in love with. So if you're attracted to girls, being a lesbian is *awesome*.

FURTHER INFORMATION AND SUPPORT

✳ Cool Page for Queer Teens: http://www.bidstrup.com/cooldat .htm

✳ National Coalition for Gay, Lesbian, Bisexual, and Transgender Youth: http://www.outproud.org

✳ National Teen and Lesbian Youth Hotline: 1-800-347-TEEN

✳ *Oasis* magazine: http://www.oasismag.com

✳ Scarleteen (information under "Gaydar"): http://www.scarleteen .com

Chapter 15

Smart Sex

Not by the Seat of Your Panties

The thing about sex is that it means making choices. The thing about choices is that it can be difficult to make the "right" ones, since you can't see into the future and know the outcome of your decisions. Basically, every decision you make is really an educated guess. And although some guesses will be *very* educated (should I wear a condom?), it's likely that others will feel more like a coin toss (do I really want to lose it to him?).

Dealing with sex and sexuality is a struggle, and you'll probably have to make important decisions at times when you're totally confused. While it's not always possible to look at all sexual situations from a rational and objective point of view, I've found it useful to always consider the following.

WHEN WONDERING WHAT TO DO, GO WITH YOUR GUT

Whenever you're doing anything sexual, you need to look out for yourself first and foremost. Be sure that you're hooking up because *you* want to, that you're enjoying the experience, and that you feel safe (both physically and emotionally). My mom always says go with your gut—if the thought of sexual intimacy with someone gives you an uneasy feeling in the pit of your stomach, take that as a warning, and don't do it.

On the other hand, if your gut is telling you to go for it, make sure you check in with the rational voice in the back of your head. The best advice I've ever gotten from a fortune cookie said, "Go with your gut, but never think that is enough." If you're gut is saying, "It's OK not to use a condom just one time," take into account the sensible part of you screaming, "No, no, no!" Your gut instinct can serve as a good warning, but when looking for the go-ahead, make sure that both your gut and your rational voice agree that it's all right.

Being rational can be difficult when you're with someone you really like and you're not totally sure how he feels about you. Some girls think that having sex with a guy is a surefire way of getting him to stick around. ("You can't leave me, you bastard—I'm sleeping with you!") But it's a mistake to think that sex will give you more control in a relationship that makes you feel powerless. More likely, it will just make you feel more vulnerable.

Other people will treat you the way that you treat yourself. If you respect your instincts and desires, a guy will respect you. No worthwhile guy will ever be less attracted to you for having or not having sex with him if it's clear that you're respecting your own needs. Have sex for you, not your friends, your boyfriend, your need to feel attractive, or anything else. Respect yourself, and be true to your feelings, and the sexual decisions you make will be good ones.

WHEN WONDERING *WHO* TO DO, MAKE SURE THAT YOU'RE COMFORTABLE

No matter how you cut it, it's impossible to have sex without having awkward moments. Sweaty bodies can make embarrassing fart noises; certain sexual positions may reveal hair in places you didn't know you had; and it can be pretty uncomfortable to explain to a guy that having no visible symptoms doesn't necessarily mean that he has disease-free genitals.

In order for you to really be able to enjoy sex (and not be mortified by any awkward situations that may arise), you need to be comfortable with the person you're having sex with. This means that if he's been diligently rubbing your pubic bone for twenty minutes, you won't be too embarrassed to say, "Actually my clitoris is about an inch lower." It means that if he asks to have sex without a condom, you can tell him no without worrying about the repercussions of disappointing him. And it means that you will be able to express your sexual and emotional needs, whatever those needs may be.

The trick to being comfortable with a partner lies in being comfortable with yourself and with your body. In order to be comfortable with your body, you may need to spend some time exploring and getting used to your vagina, figuring out what it looks like and what makes it feel good. Understand that as strange as your vagina may appear at first, it *really is* normal. You don't have to love every part of your body or think that it looks and smells perfect, but you can learn to focus on the things about it you do love and get over the things you don't.

When Deciding If It Would Be OK—Just This Once—To Not Use Protection: Keep Things in Perspective

Much of how we fantasize about sex has to do with *the moment*. But as romantic as living only for the moment may seem, your life is a lot longer than a moment (though, thanks to premature ejaculation, your early sex life may not be). When you focus only on the present, it's tempting to convince yourself that because you're *so* into this guy, and the sex is going to be *so* amazing, that you don't care if you get pregnant or an STD. But a month later, when the moment is over and you're left with a bump in your tummy or a sore in your vagina, you will care.

When you're making decisions about sex, it's important to keep things in perspective. Think about what's temporary and what's lasting. What matters now, and what will still matter years from now? In five years, will you really care what Theo thought when you said that he had to use a condom? Will it matter what that hot older guy—what was his name again?—said when you told him you weren't ready for sex? Usually, many of the things that seem to matter a lot at the time don't really mean that much within the context of the rest of your life. Any emotional drama you are dealing with now will be at most a good story to tell in a couple of years. Although your relationship with a guy can seem to be all that matters in the moment, in the long run, what really matters is your health.

As strongly as you can feel about someone, and as intoxicating as the desire to please a guy can be, unprotected sex is never worth it. Having sex without protection can have irreversible lifelong consequences, so even if it means screwing up "the moment" to protect yourself, you will always be happy you did.

WHEN DEALING WITH FEARS OR REGRETS, WORRY ABOUT THE THINGS YOU CAN CONTROL

Life is uncertain. When you walk across the street, there's a chance that you'll get hit by a car. And while you can't stop cars from barreling down the street, you can look both ways before you cross.

Sex is not without its risks. No matter how safe you are, there is always a chance that you could get pregnant or contract an STD. Then there's worrying about stereotypes, feeling emotionally vulnerable, or regretting your decisions. But it's a waste of time and too overwhelming to worry about the things you can't control—you have to worry about what you can.

You can't control the fact that one in four adolescents gets an STD each year, that condoms break, that pills fail, or that sexual assaults happen every day. What you can control is how you act and the decisions you make. If you make responsible choices, that's the best that you can do.

That said, if you haven't always made responsible choices, it's unproductive to beat yourself up over the past. That's also something that you can't control. You can't go back in time and not walk to that guy's car, or tell that man that pulling out isn't good enough. Most people, at some point in their life, make bad choices; some of them end up having bad consequences, and some of them don't. But, regardless of the outcome, you have to forgive yourself for your bad decisions and use them as insurance that you will make good ones in the future.

WHEN IN DOUBT—IT WILL (EVENTUALLY) BE OK

Sex is complicated. Enjoying it and doing it safely require trusting other people, having confidence in yourself, and fully understanding your self-worth. And at this point in your life, that's probably hard. Now is a time when you may still be a little confused about your body, guys are still intimidating, and you have not yet realized the full extent of your abilities. How do I know? Because every woman I've talked to feels more sexy, more in control, and more capable than she ever felt as a teenager or young adult.

There's really no substitution for age and experience when it comes to becoming more secure in the sex department. Having sex gets better (and less stressful) with age because you learn to become more accepting of your body and fully recognize it as a tool that can give you pleasure, not just an awkward collection of skin. Making smart sexual decisions is a no-brainer once you realize that guys, like spiders, are probably more afraid of you than you are of them. And avoiding emotionally damaging relationships is easier when you fully realize that the guy you're with is lucky to have you, and that if he doesn't respect your comfort level, there's someone else out there who will.

But the reality is, the negative consequences of having sex don't wait around until you're twenty-something and better prepared to deal with them. Although things will get easier, you're going to have to make smart decisions now—while you're still young and it's still difficult. This means that you may have to act on the blind faith that while doing the responsible thing may suck at the time, it will pay off in the long run.

I can't promise you immediate comfort and confidence with sex, but I can promise you that if you're not there yet, you'll get there eventually. I can promise that being able to recognize stereotypes will make it easier to say, "I can feel sexy and intelligent at the same time." And I can promise that knowing what to expect from sex and the sexual world is going to make everything much less confusing.

Good luck, and until it gets easier, love yourself enough to be sexually smart, and have the courage to follow your own instincts. If you're not comfortable with something, don't do it. And remember that whatever weird, awkward, or scary experiences you have had, you are not alone.

About the Author

*A*mber Madison grew up in an artists' community outside of Chapel Hill, North Carolina. She is a recent graduate of Tufts University, where she studied human sexuality and earned a degree in American Studies and Community Health. For two years she wrote a weekly column in the *Tufts Daily* about sexuality, safer sex, and relationships. *Cosmopolitan* magazine, *US News & World Report*, and other publications have profiled her in regard to her column, and her work has been featured on University Wire (www.uwire.com). Visit her online at www.ambermadisononline.com.

Index